Contents

Preface

By Hans Binnendijk and David A. Sobyra

The Center for Complex Operations (CCO) was established within the Center for Technology and National Security Policy (CTNSP) at National Defense University in February 2009. Its purpose is to address a widely perceived need for improved interagency interoperability in analysis of, planning for, and intervening in complex operations worldwide. Complex operations include reconstruction and stabilization operations, counterinsurgency, and irregular warfare—operations that must draw on all elements of national power to succeed. The goal of the CCO is to help improve the effectiveness of U.S. efforts in pursuing our national interests in complex operations, and to save lives.

Created as a collaborative initiative by the Departments of State and Defense and the United States Agency for International Development, the CCO represents a whole-of-government approach to complex operations, and embodies the "three D's" of diplomacy, defense, and development. The objectives of the CCO are to:

- Provide for effective coordination in the preparation of United States Government personnel for complex operations.
- Foster unity of effort during complex operations among
  o the departments and agencies of the United States Government,
  o foreign governments and militaries,
  o international organizations and international nongovernmental organizations, and
  o domestic non-governmental organizations.
- Conduct research; collect, analyze, and distribute lessons learned; and compile best practices in matters relating to complex operations.

- Identify gaps in the education and training of Department of Defense personnel, and other relevant United States Government personnel, relating to complex operations, and to facilitate efforts to fill such gaps.

This ambitious mandate sets a daunting agenda that must be addressed if the United States is to meet the national security challenges of the 21st century. These challenges have evolved substantially during the past two decades. The existential threat of nuclear warfare that dominated national security thinking for 50 years disappeared with the collapse of the Soviet Union. What ensued was not the global peace some had expected and many hoped for. Instead, we entered an era of diffuse and multi-dimensional threats. The enemy is not always obvious. Our national security goals are sometimes unclear. Recent experience in Iraq and Afghanistan has demonstrated the limits of our understanding of complex operations. It is critical that we continue to learn from these experiences. The CCO aims to help institutionalize the practice of effective learning from experience.

It is our hope that these essays, which represent 20 different views of complex operations, will convey some sense of the magnitude of the challenge of complex operations. The essayists include senior diplomats, development experts, and military leaders with a broad range of experience, not only from Iraq and Afghanistan, but extending back to earlier complex operations in the Balkans, Haiti, Somalia, and even Grenada. From these diverse views should emerge principles that constitute the strategic lessons of complex operations.

We would like to thank all the authors whose essays appear in this volume, as well as the many senior leaders who have pledged to support the efforts of the CCO in the future. In particular we want to recognize the efforts of Michael Miklaucic, the CCO Director of Research, Information and Dissemination, who edited this volume, and Ms. Jacqueline Carpenter, whose energy, passion and creative ideas kept the project moving. We also want to thank the CCO staff—Neyla Arnas, Nicholas Brechbill, Bernard Carreau, Dale Erickson, Christopher Maletz, Scott Moore, and Daniel Troy—without whose tireless efforts this volume would not have been possible. Finally, we would like to thank Lindsey Geddes, Scott Miller, and Robert Ooi for their dedicated support throughout this project.

Introduction

By Michael Miklaucic

The natural tendency of people to view problems from the perspective of their home organization is widely acknowledged in Washington. The corrosive effect this has on unity of intent and unity of effort is also acknowledged, documented, and lamented. As long as the stakes are small, the costs of such parochialism are apparently endurable. Our recent frustrations in Iraq and Afghanistan, however, have elevated the problem of so-called "stove-piping" to a high profile.

The proposed remedy to stove-piping is the "whole of government" approach to complex problems. Also known as the "comprehensive approach," the putative advantage of whole of government approaches is that they lift the level of analysis to a higher altitude, providing a better view of the full extent and complexity of the problem in question. The inevitable decrease in resolution, or granularity, should be more than balanced by an improved strategic perspective. Regrettably, however, the discipline of the whole of government approach has not been consistently applied, as bureaucratic inertia pushes back against proposed new practices.

Despite countless testimonials of commitment to whole of government collaboration, true collaboration remains ad hoc and dependent on specific circumstances, rather than institutionally hard-wired into the practices and behaviors of departments and agencies. Although efforts are being undertaken to improve collaboration, interagency secondments remain de-incentivized and bureaucratically cumbersome, thus discouraging the growth of a cadre of whole of government professionals. Interagency collaboration also remains stunted by incompatible communications systems, operational practices, and organizational cultures.

Complex operations, in which multiple agencies assume complementary roles and operate in close proximity—often with similar missions but conflicting mandates—accentuate these tensions. The tensions are evident in the processes of analyzing complex environments, planning for complex interventions, and implementing complex operations. Many reports and analyses forecast that these complex operations are precisely those that will demand our attention most in the indefinite future.

As essayists Barton and O'Connell note, our intelligence and understanding of the root causes of conflict, multiplicity of motivations and grievances, and dispositions of actors is often inadequate. Moreover, the problems that complex operations are intended and implemented to address are convoluted, and often inscrutable. They exhibit many if not all the characteristics of "wicked problems," as enumerated by Rittel and Webber in 1973: they defy definitive formulations; any proposed solution or intervention causes the problem to mutate, so that there is no second chance at a solution; every situation is unique; each wicked problem can be considered a symptom of another problem. As a result, policy objectives are often compound and ambiguous. The requirements of stability, for example, in Afghanistan today, may conflict with the requirements for democratic governance. Efforts to establish an equitable social contract may well exacerbate intercommunal tensions that can lead to violence. The rule of law, as we understand it, may displace indigenous conflict management and stabilization systems. Indeed, the law of unintended consequences may be the only law of the land. The complexity of the challenges we face in the current global environment would suggest the obvious benefit of joint analysis—bringing to bear on any given problem the analytic tools of military, diplomatic and development analysts. Instead, efforts to analyze jointly are most often an afterthought, initiated long after a problem has escalated to a level of urgency that negates much of the utility of deliberate planning.

In addition to good analysis, we know that effective planning is essential for the success of a complex operation. However, highly diverse planning cultures within U.S. Government agencies make effective joint planning difficult. Highlighting merely the most obvious discrepancy, the U.S. military planning culture, discipline, and capacity is not mirrored in the civilian agencies. State Department planning is, for practical purposes, limited to annual program and budget planning (using the Mission Program Planning, or MPP, tool), and the planning tools developed recently by the Office of the Coordinator for Reconstruction and Stabilization (S/CRS). The most notable product of the latter is the Interagency Management System (IMS), developed to rationalize the U.S. response to complex stabilization and reconstruction challenges. Interestingly, the IMS has never been fully tested in a real-life situation, and some doubt that it ever will be. The U.S. Agency for International Development contributes to State's annual planning exercise, in addition to its own mission country strategic plans, which, though atrophied in recent years, are generally based on a 3- or 5-year planning horizon. The recent announcement by Secretary of State Hillary Clinton of a new Quadrennial Diplomacy and Development Review (QDDR), similar to the Department of Defense Quadrennial Defense Review (QDR), indicates a step toward coordinated, if not joint, civilian-military planning. Yet, one must ask if the two processes—the QDDR and QDR—will be synchronized and collaborative. Or will the rush to create a first QDDR result in out-of-synch reviews?

Field operations are, of course, where tensions between the various organizations are most evident. The juxtaposition of fighting military forces next to humanitarian relief workers, development specialists, and diplomats can cause significant discomfort. In non-permissive environments such as Iraq and Afghanistan, military forces are called on to participate substantively and substantially in humanitarian and development efforts. Humanitarians have raised numerous issues with this participation, as have development experts. Does the provision by uniformed military of humanitarian services compromise the neutrality of humanitarian workers, and thus put them at greater risk? Does it narrow the so-called "humanitarian space?" Given the culture, training, and primary mission of military forces, is the "do no harm" philosophy embraced by many in the development and humanitarian communities viable? The U.S. military has in recent years generated a large quantity of doctrine that emphasizes the importance of the developmental and diplomatic elements of national power. The Department of Defense has even committed itself to developing whatever capacities are necessary for stabilization and reconstruction in the absence of the corresponding civilian capacity, even when a civilian agency would be a more appropriate provider. Yet, we have not explored whether the political and developmental elements of a counterinsurgency campaign are compatible with the democratization and economic elements of long-term, sustainable development.

As Ambassador James Dobbins notes in his essay, the United States has unparalleled recent experience in mounting complex operations. In the past decade, most agencies of the Federal Government have been engaged in complex operations some way or another, particularly in Iraq and Afghanistan. From this extensive experience we should have learned a great deal. But have we? George Santayana said, "those who cannot remember the past are condemned to repeat it." Chastened by our recent experiences in Iraq and Afghanistan we Americans have become obsessed with learning the lessons of the past. Lessons learned and best practices have become a growing cottage industry in the interagency community engaged in overseas complex operations. Yet, we have not institutionalized processes for articulating, validating, and disseminating lessons from past experience in complex operations. To date, the civilian departments and agencies lack a systematic approach to learning from experience, and a great deal of information, experience, learning, and, indeed, wisdom is probably lost as individuals transition to other assignments and vocations.

As acknowledged throughout the essays in this volume, the best approach to complex operations is a genuine whole of government approach. Joint analysis, planning, and implementation are appropriate, not just on the eve of a complex operation, but on a routine and habitual basis—in the pre-conflict phase as well as once conflict has begun. Yet, many barriers to effective joint collaborative analysis, planning, and implementation remain. As 9/11 recedes in memory and Iraq and Afghanistan become part of our quotidian experience in the foreign policy world, there is a risk of reverting to old habits of stove-piping and agency parochialism. Will the whole of government approach that has become so popular in response to the Iraq and Afghanistan experiences be limited to those experiences? Will the benefits of civilian-military collaboration be disregarded as agencies seek to return to more "normal" practices? Already it is possible to detect a note of impatience to do so, or of whole of government fatigue. If the insights of these essays are to be trusted, as I believe on the whole they should be, failure to firmly institutionalize a whole of government philosophy and associated practices would be a lamentable mistake, and would constitute an unforgiveable failure to learn the lessons of our experience.

Essay 1

Command in Afghanistan 2003–2005: Three Key Lessons Learned

By David Barno

The operational experience and lessons learned described in this article result from my 19 months as the overall commander of U.S. and coalition forces in Afghanistan from 2003–2005. As the senior U.S. commander, I held geographic responsibilities to U.S. Central Command for a sub-region that included all of Afghanistan, most of Pakistan, and the southern portions of Uzbekistan and Tajikistan—a four-country joint operations area. My first task upon arrival in theater was to establish a new three-star headquarters in Kabul from the ground up, while concurrently assuming overall command of ongoing training and combat operations across the entire area of operations. This unique opportunity provided a host of "lessons learned" stemming from a set of challenges few other commanders at that time faced. My command responsibilities spanned a set of tasks best described on the spectrum of operations as reaching from theater-strategic/pol-mil through the high end of the operational level; my subordinate two-star combined joint task force held tactical and lower end operational level responsibilities across our battlespace.

Three key lessons pertaining to strategic and operational command in irregular warfare during this demanding period stand out. First, focusing on the big picture: strategy not tactics, winning not simply battles, but the war became the central task. Second, the vital importance of integrating the civil-military effort, beginning at the most senior levels, was crucial to success. Finally, the essential task of communicating and building relationships of trust with key players of disparate backgrounds was a prerequisite to achieving effective results. Each of these topics is worthy of an extensive discussion, but this piece will attempt to summarize the most salient points related to each.

Focusing on the big picture seems an obvious principle to promote at the senior level of military command. Unfortunately, the U.S. Army's cultural predisposition toward "war-fighting" (fighting and winning battles) versus "war-winning" (bringing conflicts to a successful conclusion) remains a powerful influence affecting theater level leadership, so emphasizing the primacy of the big picture deserves strong reinforcement.

Senior commanders are drawn from an environment that rewards tactical level performance. Successful two-star division commanders are drawn from successful colonels and brigadiers who have proven their mettle not as strategic leaders, but as master tacticians. Three- and four-star leaders are chosen from successful two-star commanders—thus a predilection toward the importance of tactical performance is reinforced by our promotion and selection system. Senior commanders are often unwittingly pulled toward operating and prioritizing in ways that have delivered success in their career—a dynamic that often works at cross purposes with the need to understand leadership in new ways, which is the sine qua non of successful operational and strategic command.

Moreover, despite the central civil-military dynamic that defines effective counterinsurgency, the temptation for the U.S. military to "go it alone" and conduct military operations not fully harmonized with civil action remains a challenge—and one played out on several occasions in Afghanistan from 2002-2008. "War-fighting" may not always require civil players to achieve success—"battles" are won, after all, by soldiers—but the much more complex notion of "war-winning" almost always requires a whole of government approach. Successful counterinsurgency campaigns, in the famous characterization of French COIN expert David Galula, are often 80 percent non-military and only 20 percent military.[1]

Focusing on the big picture requires a clear understanding of the policy goals that the military effort is designed to serve. In most cases

---

[1] David Galula, *Counterinsurgency Warfare: Theory and Practice* (Westport, CT: Praeger Security International, 1964).

those goals will not be simply military in nature; some degree of interagency (and sometimes, international) effort will be required to achieve most policy objectives. This presents military commanders with a dilemma: how much should they get involved outside the military sphere? Commanders will not "command" many of the interagency actors whose combined actions will be needed to achieve the policy goals handed down from Washington. Conversely, in such situations, military leaders may not be held fully accountable for the outcome. Do military commanders simply "stay in their lane," work on the military and security lines of operation, and define their mission statement narrowly to deliver the "military requirement?" Or do commanders extend their horizons, seek maximum flexibility in their mission statements, leverage their military capacity (nearly always the biggest resource available), and drive their organization toward a broader set of whole-of-government policy goals to enable the overarching policy objectives to be met?

From 2003–2005 in Afghanistan, my approach was the latter. As I shared with an overworked staff officer in my headquarters in late 2003, "We own it all." This outlook was strikingly different from the approach taken by previous commanders (likely operating under other guidance). Previous commanders had limited interaction with the civilian leadership and were operating from a military headquarters that was a 90-minute drive outside the capital of Kabul. In fact, my orders in standing up a new headquarters were explicitly to position it in Kabul and build closer connections with the U.S. embassy and newly arriving U.S. ambassador. This guidance was in belated recognition that (by 2003 at least) geographically separating the U.S. civilian and military leadership during a prolonged engagement in Afghanistan was not a productive approach.

Creating a unified, civil-military approach was a second major challenge. Fortunately, our new U.S. ambassador, Zalmay Khalilzad, fully understood this necessity and became an ideal partner in this formidable task. Personalities matter immensely in conditions of crisis, and ours meshed—no small bit of good fortune! Our staffs began to recognize that there would be no seams or "white space" between the U.S. ambassador and the senior military commander, and that expectations were being set for strongly integrated efforts between the two organizations. I understood that if the U.S. military "succeeded" in Afghanistan—won every tactical engagement, killed more of the

Taliban—yet the U.S. embassy failed—could not facilitate a nation-wide presidential election, could not complete the Ring Road project, failed to disarm and separate warlords—the overall mission would fail, and U.S. policy goals would not be achieved. This was a fundamental realization that quickly began to shape all of our military endeavors.

The implementation of a unified civil-military approach took a myriad of forms. My day began and ended at the U.S. embassy (where I also resided in a half-trailer)—to better encounter the ambassador at off moments. The first 2 hours of the day included meetings with the ambassador for country team meetings (to demonstrate our one-team approach) and security core group meetings to cross talk among all the senior U.S. military and interagency players in Afghanistan and synchronize directions. U.S. military officers were seconded to many embassy offices, and five senior military planners were provided to the ambassador to form an "Embassy Interagency Planning Group" that would provide strategic planning for the ambassador and devise metrics and performance measures for the overall U.S. mission in Afghanistan. Ambassador Khalilzad and I would often travel together to key events outside Kabul, and we attended all openings of provincial reconstruction teams (PRTs) together. This close relationship paid us both huge dividends and was a benchmark for our military and diplomatic organizations (Defense coming from "Mars" and State from "Venus"), clearly demonstrating the expectations for close and supportive relations at all levels.

Communicating and building relationships with actors of all different backgrounds was another critical lesson learned. Military officers are raised and schooled in environments consisting largely of other military officers. The political-military environment of senior command in Afghanistan was anything but military in nature. As the commander of U.S. Central Command, General John Abizaid, noted in his concise initial guidance to me: "Your job, Dave, is big Pol and little Mil," alluding to the scope of the political-military challenge and the priorities needed in our new approach. To implement this guidance, I began to spend large portions of my time interacting with the many actors in Kabul who significantly influenced the overall international effort in Afghanistan. They too would have immense impact on the success or failure of U.S. policy objectives—whether Afghan ministers, ambassadors from NATO nations, or key UN officials.

Key to achieving some degree of synergy of effort between this diverse set of players were personal relationships. I began to realize early in my tenure that building a personal relationship with each of these key individuals—something which extended beyond simply good manners in office calls—became a "force multiplier," in military parlance, and created a wellspring of good will and trust that might be of substantial future importance. Mutual trust became an essential ingredient to resolving thorny and contentious issues that were inherent in the international effort in Kabul.

A salient example of the importance of trust-building was the relationship that evolved between the U.S. military and the United Nations in Afghanistan. On a personal level, this was embodied in the relationship that developed between the U.S. military commander and the Senior Representative of the UN Secretary General (SRSG). Institutionally, these two organizations were highly dissimilar—in some ways from opposing cultures, and populated by dedicated and committed individuals of very different backgrounds who largely viewed each other with suspicion. Given the central importance of the UN mission in Afghanistan to the legitimacy of the international mission, as well as to the looming first-ever Afghan presidential election, an uncooperative or contentious relationship between the UN and the U.S. military was fraught with peril.

At his invitation, the SRSG, Jean Arnault, and I began to have breakfast every Monday morning at his residence. A Frenchman who was a career diplomat, Jean was of dramatically different background and interests than any American general. Yet, these informal get-togethers produced not only useful discussions on issues of mutual importance, but laid the foundation for an increasingly strong personal connection between Mr. Arnault and myself—one that continues to this day. We grew to trust each other and to clearly see where our two organizations had much in common as we looked to the desired outcome in Afghanistan. Moreover, we intuitively realized that neither of our organizations could accomplish its objectives without the help of the other.

The importance of a genuine relationship of shared trust and confidence between two leaders of different organizations was immense. Just as with the institutional diplomatic-military benefits accruing to my ties to the U.S. ambassador, SRSG Arnault's and my organizations (the UN mission and the U.S. military) quickly began to understand that "the bosses got along" and would not brook the "staff wars" that often endanger good relations between institutions with different outlooks and missions. Conversely, the close relationship between the two senior leaders fostered an environment in which subordinates could take broad initiatives on a host of issues knowing that over-arching institutional goals and objectives were shared. When a crisis might erupt in Afghanistan that threatened the security of international aid workers—four Médecins Sans Frontières physicians were murdered in early 2004, and MSF left the country—our personal relationship of trust helped both the United States and the UN evaluate the threat and react in ways that, absent that personal relationship, might have caused the UN to shut down key parts of its vital operations across Afghanistan.

Relationships of mutual respect and confidence with host-nation counterparts are equally crucial in an irregular warfare environment. My senior leader engagements regularly took me to meet with the Chief of General Staff of the Afghan National Army (ANA), General Bismullah Khan. General Bismullah was a Tajik and former mujahid who had fought the Soviets and then the Taliban for his entire adult life. Though only in his mid-40s, he was prematurely aged by long, hard fighting. He spoke always through an interpreter, which further complicated dialogue. That said, we struck a very close relationship and built close ties between our two organizations. Our discussions over tea in his office were always wide-ranging and often very indirect. The highest compliment I ever received from an Afghan came from Bismullah after I has returned to the United States: "(General Barno) never told us what to do in our meetings, but when he left the office, we always knew what he wanted us to do." Indirection and respect for cultural norms had a powerful influence when coming from a commander whose forces were in very real terms guests within the sovereign nation of Afghanistan.

In sum, my "lessons learned" boil down to this: theater level command in an irregular warfare setting demands a broader set of skills than those required of conventional war at the same level. Some basic questions arise as to whether our selection and development of senior officers for command in this environment adequately recognize this fact. Our military leaders today are superbly trained and equipped by their lifelong experience to lead difficult military contingency operations anywhere in the world. Where they may fall short is in understanding the leadership requirements across the increasingly important non-military sphere and their centrality to success in irregular warfare.

Lack of civil resources in most conflict settings will demand that military leaders and their organizations play a very large role in the non-military dimension of irregular warfare and stability operations. Senior military leaders have limited experience and often even less preparation for this role—although 8 years of war in Iraq and Afghanistan have now provided some hard-won knowledge that is slowly becoming more common at senior levels. More and more, senior commanders must clearly see the big picture, understand how the military can engage to deliver whole-of-government policy objectives to achieve strategic ends, and possess the personal and cross-cultural skills to build relationships of trust with key actors outside the military sphere. In today's environment of prolonged complex contingencies, these talents are paramount requirements for overall success. We need to closely examine whether our process of educating, developing, and selecting our senior military leaders can meet this strategic leadership challenge.

Understanding the Situation

By Frederick Barton

As the Kosovo situation worsened in late 1998, USAID's Office of Transition Initiatives received a call from Secretary of State Madeleine Albright's office. Her aide, Jim O'Brien, asked if there were opportunities to engage the population and political leaders as part of an effort to avoid war with Serbia.

Within 2 weeks, ten or so American field organizers, diplomats and political development professionals were sent into Kosovo to see what options might be available. On arrival in Pristina, the team broke up into sub-teams of two that moved into a handful of cities throughout the province. For the next few weeks, each sub-team met with hundreds of Kosovo residents, gauged their anxieties and enthusiasms, and searched for community initiatives that might engage the population.

About the same time, the U.S. National Security Council began a regular series of Deputies meetings on Kosovo in the basement of the White House. At least once a week, the Deputy National Security Adviser, Jim Steinberg, would convene a group that included the number two persons from State, DOD, the Joint Chiefs, the CIA, and the chair of USAID's working group on Kosovo, plus a few others. Each meeting would start with a 5-minute CIA review of the situation on the ground. The mood in the room and the discussion often followed the information and the tone of that initial briefing.

When the USAID team returned to Washington, I spoke with the CIA briefer right after a Deputies meeting. "I don't know what assets you have on the ground in Kosovo, but we have a team that just spent a month in every part of the province and we would be happy to share their insights." "We would be delighted to hear their report," my CIA colleague said, "since we don't have anyone on the ground in Kosovo."

Here we were, just weeks before a likely war[1] in an area that is smaller than Connecticut, and our intelligence was limited to electronic surveillance and aerial images. On a cloudy day, America's ability to monitor the movement of Serbian tanks was denied. At least the overt USAID operatives were able to feel the ground shake when heavy vehicles drove by their guest houses. It seemed hard to imagine that we could not be better informed, especially when lives were at risk.

My experience has confirmed that poor intelligence is more the rule than the exception. America's analysis of countries in conflict is not good, and there are not many nations that do it better. Examples of inadequacy abound: the UN Department of Political Affairs is notoriously understaffed, and also reluctant to provoke a collapsing member state with gloomy reports; lead countries, such as France in Cote d'Ivoire, seem to be more proprietary than analytical when a crisis looms; even Israel, with its sophisticated systems and thousands of human contacts, can still be surprised when it ventures into a tiny geographic area like Gaza.

What are some of the chronic shortcomings?

First, there is a reluctance to anticipate. Almost all experts failed to anticipate the rapid collapse of the Soviet Union before the Berlin Wall fell in 1989, despite academies full of sovietologists. Hamas' success in the Palestinian elections of 2005 shocked another set of experts. More recently, the Taliban advance to within 60 miles of Pakistan's capitol, Islamabad, surprised Washington and produced a crisis mentality.

Not only are there numerous early warning systems and reports,[2] but much of the daily international news highlights disturbing trends. One of my favorite bosses, former USAID Assistant Administrator Doug Stafford, used to say, "Give me the Reuters wire and I will be able to tell you where the next humanitarian crisis will be." Today, Reuters is abetted by blogs, email, and cellular communications, but these

---

[1] For more information, see Tim Judah, *Kosovo: What Everyone Needs to Know* (New York: Oxford University Press, 2008).

[2] Frederick Barton and Karin von Hippel, with Sabina Sequeira and Mark Irvine, *Early Warning? A Review of Conflict Prediction Models and Systems*, Center for Strategic and International Studies, Post Conflict Reconstruction Project special report, available at <http://forums.csis.org/pcrproject/?page_id=267>.

resources have not initiated a rush to prepare. Overload may now be another reason to miss the obvious.

Denial remains the norm. While many will embrace the longer-term predictions of massive and expensive studies by the intelligence community,[3] or rush to the emergency of the day, there is a seeming inability to take the next step and prepare for the crisis of tomorrow. A conversation with one of the wisest UN officials about developing problems in Pakistan around 2002 serves as a good example. "Pakistan cannot collapse," he said. When asked, "Why not?," his response was, "Because it would be too awful!"

Of course there are numerous other reasons to resist a thoughtful approach, including the usual refuge of scoundrels, the shibboleth of sovereignty. By playing that card, miserable leaders can deflect international attention and rally nationalist zeal behind their destructive patterns. Americans can use the inverse argument to say it is outside our jurisdiction.

Equally distressing are more mundane hazards: a lack of imagination; overly busy scheduling of policymakers; and a cloying possessiveness by those responsible for a place or problem within the bureaucracy. As a colleague recently wrote, "Both parts are debilitating; first the principals are so time-pressed that they are often tempted by the meretricious call of the glibbest arguments, if argued forcefully enough; and, the bureaucratic infighting is endemic."

Efforts have been made to address these patterns, but they have not gained the upper hand. Under USAID Administrator Andrew Natsios, the new Office of Conflict Mitigation and Management,[4] which was founded in 2002, began a series of conflict assessment reports that detailed the volatility of 20 countries. A valuable innovation, the reports were seen to be too controversial, ended up being tightly held, and have been cut back to a few per year. Their wise intent was to guide future programming to address the central political development

---

[3] National Intelligence Council, *Mapping the Global Future: Report of the National Intelligence Council's 2020 Project*, available at <http://www.dni.gov/nic/NIC_2020_project html>.

[4] Office of Conflict Mitigation and Management, United States Agency for International Development, available at <http://www.usaid.gov/our_work/cross-cutting_programs/conflict/>.

challenges facing many nations. The State Department's best diplomatic reporting should do this, too, but it often addresses the more immediate time horizon. Similarly, the often-touted country war plans of the Pentagon are unlikely to have the granularity or political insight that helps with anticipation.

Second, these are tough places to work. The qualities that have brought a country to conflict are intimidating at most levels, including physical danger, closed societies, mafia-like infestations, oppressive and exploitive leadership, and widespread corruption. All of these elements conspire to produce a noxious blend of misinformation and disinformation and a diet of anecdotes that are heavy on rumors and conspiracy theories.

The current situation in Pakistan provides a good example. With the top government leadership having been traded back and forth between a handful of civilians and the military for nearly 50 years, almost every description of a top-level player is framed in some version of near character assassination.

How can you figure out what is going on when so few people feel safe enough to speak the truth?

In the late 1990s the U.S. Government led a well-intentioned effort to address impunity in Burundi. A resolution was passed at the UN, and recruiting of an international panel of justice experts was initiated. When the USAID Office of Transition Initiatives (USAID/OTI) was approached by the State Department for core funding to support this worthy human rights cause, a fundamental question was asked: who will protect the witnesses or the prosecutors, since impunity continues to be a core problem in Burundi?

At the behest of USAID/OTI, a small team of proponents of the idea flew to Bujumbura to assess conditions on the ground before any financial commitment would be made. While they had planned a 2-week investigation, the trip was cut short after a few days because, as one team member said, "We could have been killed!" The project did not proceed.

In Haiti, the brazen midday assassination in 1993 of Justice Minister Guy Malary—a high-ranking official who was seeking to move beyond the tyranny of intimidation—marked a turning point in American understanding of that nation's long reign of terror. His murder could not have been more audacious.

Many of the practices of the international community do not help. "Safety first" and "force protection is job one" policies often limit diplomats and soldiers to compounds, bases, and familiar places. Investing scarce dollars in the construction of isolated and forbidding new U.S. embassies does not foster the flow of information.[5]

During my work on the Smart Power Commission,[6] I asked American audiences to make the following choice: "Would you prefer to spend $500 million on the construction of a new Embassy in Baghdad or the same amount to prepare and train 500 Americans to work in the region with full language, history, and social skills?" Of several hundred people in multiple settings who raised their hands, only a handful favored the Embassy.

We have not yet figured out how to strike the right institutional balance between caution and a firsthand feeling for a situation, though there are many exceptions. The provincial reconstruction teams in Afghanistan and Iraq have tried to do this, along with Special Forces and Marine Corps units in multiple places. The "surge" strategy in Iraq was defined by the placement of soldiers in the communities versus on bases or in garrisons, and there are thousands of civilians, many with non-governmental organizations (NGOs) who work at extraordinary risk "outside the wire."

Success will demand a more thoughtful and mutually agreed upon risk profile, otherwise field reporting is little different than observations that can be made from a desk in the United States.

Third, there is a strong predisposition to rely on conventional wisdom. Dependence on familiar sources or experts, an attraction to popular narratives, an inability to appreciate the dynamics of conflict-prone situations, and a tendency to exaggerate what we know all influence analysis. An April 2008 visit to Quetta in the Baluchistan area of Pakistan confirmed how these habits can produce a confused picture. As we interviewed dozens of people, the range of information

---

[5] "Report on the Embassy of the Future," Center for Strategic and International Studies, <http://csis.org/files/media/csis/pubs/embassy_of_the_future.pdf>.
[6] CSIS Smart Power Initiative, "Dialogue with America," Center for Strategic and International Studies, available at <http://www.csis.org/smartpower/>.

gathered made it clear that it would be nearly impossible to describe the situation with much confidence. We heard that there were 800 foreign fighters or 10,000; that they were integrated into the community including marrying locals or were violent outsiders who were beheading people; that the Uzbeks were the most extreme, or were part of a multi-generational group that had a row of car mechanic shops in Quetta; that the military and the ISI were double-dealing and actually responsible for most of the attacks; and that the drone attacks were now hitting more foreign fighters (an acceptable result for most Pakistanis).

And the stories went on. Most of those we spoke with had valid personal insights, but only small pieces of a hugely complex puzzle. Surely, hundreds of local sources would be needed, and their information would have to be cross-checked and filtered, often outside familiar channels, to better understand the violence in the region.

As CSIS began to work on Pakistan in 2005, it became clear that several critical elements were missing, including a clear sense of how much the United States was spending and on what. Surprisingly, there was no single repository for that information at the Office of Management and Budget, the Appropriations Committees, or the national security agencies. At a gathering of regional experts, we asked for estimates of the figure; the consensus was $750 million per year. When it was suggested that the number was closer to $2 billion per year, there was a howl of rejection. A similar exchange occurred with Ambassador Ryan Crocker in Islamabad. The detailed release of the numbers has altered the debate.[7]

A more recent roundtable on the Democratic Republic of the Congo (DRC) reached a familiar story line. One of the experts at the table decried the lack of international commitment to the DRC. Interrupting the discussion, the group was asked, what is the level of financial contribution? Within a few minutes, 15 experts had agreed that it was close to $3 billion per year, half for peacekeeping forces and a significant portion for emergency food. The narrative changed from "not enough" to "how could we spend this more effectively."

---

[7] Craig Cohen, "A Perilous Course: U.S. Strategy and Assistance to Pakistan," A Report of the Post-Conflict Reconstruction Project, Center for Strategic and International Studies, August 2007, available at <http://csis.org/blog/new-pcr-report-perilous-course-us-strategy-and-assistance-pakistan>.

The political analysis of conflict cases is also often warped. Take Haiti prior to the U.S. invasion in 1994. With an excessive reliance on familiar sources, most international observers missed the rapid emergence of Father Bertrand Aristide in the 1990 elections and were stunned by his first-round election victory over a large field of established candidates. As he sat in Washington in exile, the victim of one more coup, Aristide continued to be victimized by time-worn analysis and characterized by some as a dangerous radical. Those who were neither supporters nor opponents of Aristide were assumed to be in the middle, and therefore the moderates, and that perception shaped America's official analysis. The two graphics below show the original interpretation and the one that eventually led to the U.S. intervention of 1994.

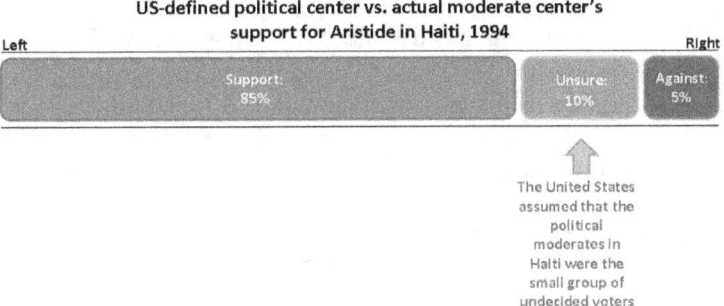

Once U.S. policy began to acknowledge that the middle of the bar was representative of the moderate voices of Haiti, the logic for supporting the restoration of the freely elected President grew. As the following graphic became real, the discussion changed and the "immaculate invasion" took place.[8]

---

[8] See Bob Shacochis, *The Immaculate Invasion,* (New York: Viking Press, 1999).

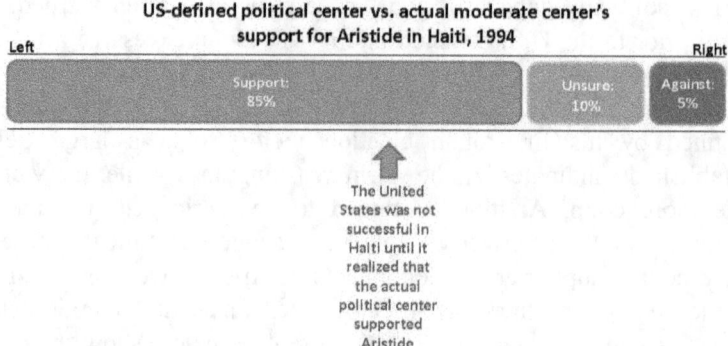

US-defined political center vs. actual moderate center's support for Aristide in Haiti, 1994

Left   Right

Support: 85%   Unsure: 10%   Against: 5%

The United States was not successful in Haiti until it realized that the actual political center supported Aristide

American official analysis of Pakistan is largely driven by the primacy in the minds of policymakers of U.S. troops in Afghanistan. Until recently, most Americans who visited Pakistan traveled from Islamabad toward Afghanistan, and the dominant view of Pakistan was driven by progress in the war in Afghanistan. The significance of the war in Afghanistan made it difficult for U.S. analysts to develop an independent view of equally serious events in Pakistan. As Pakistan moved into crisis and its importance to American interests grew, the Pakistan portfolio at State and DOD remained weak. For a while, a single, talented, intelligence analyst at State was responsible for Pakistan—along with Nepal. At DOD, a vital regional post turned over three times in less than a year. The result was a view of Pakistan in an Afghan context. For an outsider, it was striking how much the analysis differed from Kabul to Lahore.

A similar effect was evident in the Congo and Rwanda in the 1990s, after the genocide and the collapse of the 32 year-long dictatorial rule of Mobutu. The views of those who worked in Kinshasa versus those in Kigali were dramatically different—and one could detect the origin of the argument within the first minute of conversation.

Even with an in-depth understanding of the community, it is hard to sort out a situation. Prior to the genocide in Rwanda, the U.S. Ambassador was Dave Rawson, a career diplomat who had spent much of his childhood in the region as the son of a Methodist missionary doctor, spoke Kinyarwanda, and had numerous unofficial contacts in various parts of the country. He loved his work and the people of the region and felt blessed to be working on a political solution to the long-term division through direct involvement in regional peace talks.

Dedicated, sincere, and humble, Rawson was a near-perfect fit for the job.

Despite these great strengths, the ambassador may have missed the most devastating developing story—the genocide. Perhaps he was too hopeful about the peace talks. Maybe he was a prisoner of his own great knowledge. Almost surely, he was part of a tiny universe of U.S. government experts, working in semi-isolation on a non-strategic part of the world, who did not enjoy much support or the engagement of senior leadership.

In a recent Georgetown report, Janne Nolan observed that:

> The case studies reveal a consistent weakness of U.S. strategy in engaging other countries at the local and regional level. Each case demonstrates how the prevailing concept of U.S. strategic interests is defined in a way to overshadow the importance of understanding "conditions on the ground." This appears to be true whether or not the United States is maintaining an active presence in the country or region.[9]

In conflict cases, no one has a view of the whole, and the pieces of the picture must be assembled painstakingly. These are not moments for a rush to judgment. It is hard to charge ahead when the base of information is soft. Reluctance, skepticism, even subversion of conventional wisdom is advisable, especially when lives are so much at risk.

Suggestions

This paper has tried to suggest alternative methods and models throughout, but a few final suggestions might be helpful.

Start with an inclusive and expansive model that consults with all available regional experts, and then broadens into an integrated "wisdom of crowds" model.[10] If the process is broad enough, ranging

---

[9] Janne E. Nolan, *Diplomacy and Security in the Twenty-first Century* (Washington, DC: Institute for the Study of Diplomacy, School of Foreign Service, Georgetown University, 2009), available at <http://isd.georgetown.edu/diplomacy_and_security.pdf>.

[10] James Surowiecki, *The Wisdom of Crowds: Why the Many Are Smarter Than the Few and How Collective Wisdom Shapes Business, Economies, Societies and Nation* (New York: Doubleday, 2004).

from focus groups to surveys and structured conversations, including everyone from elementary school students to former Presidents, there should be some weight of the evidence that will at least allow a mostly accurate first impression of the situation. Conflict cases are best understood as "impressionism," rather than the detailed, "Grand Master" precision.

Sometimes these impressions are perfectly encapsulated by one interview. I remember the first U.S. ambassador with whom we worked in Angola saying, "On the one hand we have a murderer (Savimbi) and on the other a thief (Dos Santos), and the U.S. has decided to go with the thief."

Spend plenty of time in the place with guides you trust. There is no substitute for personal impressions, live contact with people, and the time to digest local opinions in the press, on TV, or in conversations. Curiosity is the key to sound analysis, and if it is not boundless, then the work will not be valuable.

Use a multi-dimensional and interdisciplinary form of analysis. Conflict is a wicked witch's brew of human failings and depravity, so expand the references well beyond economics, power politics, ethnic groupings, religion, and many of the other shorthand explanations. If all of the optics are used, and the situation is seen as part sociology, political science, economics, popular culture and more, then the analysis is more likely to be sound.

Encourage "red teams" and other regular challenges of conclusions at every level of the process. Make sure that access is never denied and that the rewards for questioning are visible and significant. The Army has formally instituted this practice, but already there are reports of its marginalization.

The story of retired three-star Marine Corps General Paul van Riper told in Malcolm Gladwell's *Blink* should be instructive.[11] As the Pentagon prepared a $250 million dollar war game exercise that would confirm the effectiveness of new technologies in a Gulf state environment, van Riper was charged with playing the part of America's

---

[11] Malcolm Gladwell, *Blink: The Power of Thinking Without Thinking,* (New York: Little, Brown and Company, 2005).

local opponent. Within a day, he had managed to destroy many of the U.S. advantages and produced a halt in the exercise.[12]

Opportunities to improve analysis abound in most big government or big bureaucracy settings.

Conclusion

With a genuine desire for first-rate preparation, successful conflict and stabilization operations are possible. If anticipation, analysis, and understanding the context are short-changed, the results will be tragic.

During the run-up to the 1994 Haiti invasion, Marine General Jack Sheehan questioned a gathering of senior U.S. government officials about the state of readiness for the operation. As reports were delivered from around the table, a certain amount of grade inflation, perhaps even bravado, set in. Sensing that, Sheehan said, "Gentlemen (the group was all male), that is the kind of preparation that gets young Americans killed." He was right to challenge all of us to do better.

---

[12] Fred Kaplan, "War-Gamed: Why the Army shouldn't be so surprised by Saddam's moves," *Slate*, March 28, 2003, available at <http://www.slate.com/id/2080814/>.

Reflections on Post-Conflict Politics of Reform: a Voice from Inside Iraq

By Nesreen Barwari

In October 1981, at the age of 14, I was thrown into one of Saddam Hussein's political prisons. At 24, I was a refugee, struggling for survival on Iraq's Turkish border. A decade later, in 2003, I became the only woman to hold a cabinet post in Iraq's first post-Saddam government. Defying the typical Middle Eastern stereotype for what women should and could do, my career to date has been a seamless series of opportunities sought to improve the human condition, with full-spectrum involvement, from local environments to senior levels of responsibility at regional and national levels. I headed up the United Nations reconstruction project in the Kurdistan Region of Iraq after the Gulf War; after earning a Masters Degree in Public Policy and Management from Harvard's Kennedy School. I later led the Kurdistan Regional Government's reconstruction of 3,000 destroyed villages.

In September 2003, appointed by the Coalition Provisional Authority (CPA) and under the guidance of the Iraqi Governing Council (IGC), I inherited a devastated ministry of 45,000 employees, 100,000 properties, and innumerable pieces of public works' machinery in various states of serviceability. Throughout the country in over 250 municipalities where most Iraqis reside, the Ministry of Municipalities and Public Works was responsible for drinking water supply, management of environmental sanitation services (sewerage and solid waste), and urban planning and development.

As Iraq's Minister of Municipalities and Public Works I led the renovation of ministry facilities that had been thoroughly looted and trashed, reorientation and reinvigoration of demoralized and disaffected staff, and modernization of outdated systems. In a highly politicized environment, and under formidable personal and security threats and severe resource constraints, we tried to maintain and advance public services to the extent possible. Among many examples, my ministry took a lead role in restoring essential public services following highly destructive armed conflict in the cities of Najaf and Fallujah.

During my three ministerial appointments in Baghdad, I attracted attention and resources to ongoing works and development activities to strengthen responsiveness toward improving the delivery of essential public services. I also introduced measures to promote public ethics and integrity in ministry contracts and operations. In addition to my ministerial duties and responsibilities, I took a lead role in matters pertaining to women's affairs, most notably in a much publicized overturning of an Iraqi Governing Council (IGC) resolution that would have severely diminished women's rights. I set out to convince the IGC of the vital role women should play in rebuilding the country and helped introduce, working with women NGOs, a quota system that required that all Iraqi representative bodies include at least 25 percent women.

Transitioning from a traumatic past to a promising future did not just happen. Not so long ago, many who are leaders in Iraq today were insurgents fighting a despotic regime. Governing through crises has been a regular feature of Iraq since 2003. It hasn't always been handled well. There have indeed been inadequate capacities, shortcomings, mistakes, and missteps. But there have also been many successes.

The overthrow of Saddam Hussein's regime in April 2003 was a milestone in my country's history. For decades. the people of Iraq had faced acute uncertainty to the point where too many, especially among the youth, resigned themselves to having no future. The initiative to minimize and reduce hardship for the people of Iraq led to effective action on the part of all involved—the Iraqi people, the U.S.-led coalition forces, UN agencies, and international NGOs and the governments and publics who supported them. With the support of international organizations, the leadership in Iraq, despite internal differences and lack of administrative experience, rose to the occasion.

The new Iraqi government's first challenges were to suppress terrorism and develop Iraq's security services; build a democratic, free Iraq; revive Iraq's economy; encourage entrepreneurship and enterprise establish adequate safety nets for the less privileged; and achieve economic rehabilitation, which required some tough and unpopular changes, such as the reduction of government subsidies.

Creating a functioning Iraqi economy out of failed state economic structures was a daunting task. A host of thorny challenges persisted, such as: difficulty in restarting vital public services, particularly power and water; out-of-work civil servants and former soldiers; Iraq's crushing international debt burden; a number of state-owned industries that were not market competitive; a literacy rate that had been falling for decades; infrastructure in need of serious investment; shortages of gas (for cars and cooking) and other key supplies; and a population that is predominantly young.

The immediate needs were to provide short-term employment opportunities to keep people off the streets and to refurbish basic services, such as electricity, water, and sanitation, to avoid exacerbating political and security problems.

No one questions that almost 12 years of sanctions in Iraq inflicted tremendous suffering on the Iraqi people. Coming in the wake of those sanctions, the regime change in April 2003 took place at a moment of unprecedented vulnerability for millions of Iraqis. We faced many obstacles, including security conditions that offered little freedom to operate and a basic social infrastructure, such as water, electricity, and accessibility, that was in deplorable condition. Iraqi professionals were doing their jobs at considerable personal risk, and some gave their lives to this mission. Their compassion is to be celebrated. Even compassion has a context, however, and this one is extremely complex. Relief and reconstruction in Iraq took place against the backdrop of a military occupation.

Iraq's reconstruction process needed to take place in a way that respected the long-denied basic human rights of all Iraqis. In addition, a progressive humanitarian agenda had to recognize the critical importance of encouraging local initiative in the rebuilding of the country, thereby strengthening an emerging Iraqi civil society.

Rebuilding Iraq was an enormous task. The first 12 months were decisive; the early months were crucial to turning around the security situation, which was volatile in key parts of the country.

Iraqi ownership of the rebuilding process needed to be expanded at national, provincial, and local levels while public safety was established throughout the country. Idle hands needed to be put to work, and basic economic and social services extended immediately to avoid exacerbating political and security problems. Short-term public works projects were needed on a large scale to soak up sizable amounts of the available labor pool. A massive public works rehabilitation program in all provinces helped to spur wide-ranging economic activity and empower key agents of change, including women. Immediate refurbishment of basic services, especially electricity, water, and sanitation, was urgently needed. Decentralization was essential. The job facing occupation and Iraqi authorities was too big to be handled exclusively by the central occupying authority and the IGC. Implementation lagged far behind needs and expectations in key areas, in part because of severely constrained human resources at the provincial and local levels.

Prewar Assumptions

The original U.S. plan for establishing an Iraqi government could not be implemented after the bureaucratic and administrative structures had collapsed and looting had destroyed government ministries. Further, the lack of accurate information about the state of Iraqi society and infrastructure led to overly optimistic projections. Prior to Operation *Iraqi Freedom*, the historical evidence was that looting was typical in immediate postwar environments. It would have been useful if coalition planners had anticipated looting and devised a contingency plan. Even if the plan had proven imperfect, the process of planning would have better prepared the coalition for establishing governing structures.

Lack of prewar planning left coalition forces and their civilian counterparts without the resources or policy guidance needed to stabilize and reconstruct Iraq. The State Department's "Future of Iraq" Project considered the wider aspects of Iraqi nation-building. (I participated in four Future of Iraq Project workshops in Washington, DC, between October 2002 and February 2003.) The project was especially noteworthy in that it brought together scores of Iraqi opposition figures in 2002 and early 2003 to examine how Iraqi politics, society, and government institutions could be reformed after the removal of Saddam's regime. This process usefully assembled many of the Iraqi intellectuals and opposition activists who were to be involved in post-Saddam politics, and addressed many of the political and institutional issues that would have to be considered. However, although the project enabled the U.S. government to expand its contacts with Iraqi exiles, its product was disregarded as a result of the decision to give the exclusive lead for postwar reconstruction to DOD. Dismissing this effort and others by non-DOD departments was a significant postwar mistake.

DOD planners and the Iraqi expatriates they engaged and later deployed into Iraqi institutions were hampered by assumptions that were to prove faulty: that military operations would have a clear and decisive end (i.e., there would not be extensive postwar resistance by Iraqi forces); that the coalition would have to deal with serious humanitarian crises, including flows of refugees and internally displaced people; that the coalition could rapidly hand over civil governance to robust Iraqi governing institutions such as the line ministries and the police; and that most Iraqis would embrace the political transition to a "new Iraq" and actively support democratization of the political system.

Postwar Reality

The reality of postwar Iraq was different. The first surprise was the absence of major humanitarian crises. This was in part attributable to the rapid collapse of the Saddam regime, which had in any case handed out rations prior to the hostilities. The second surprise was the disintegration and paralysis of governing institutions, notably law and order structures. While a certain amount of disorder and criminality had been predicted, the surprise was the complete disappearance of Iraqi security institutions during April 2003. Prewar planners had assumed that the Interior Ministry and Iraqi police would take the lead in ensuring public safety, and that some formed Iraqi army units would be available to assist with maintaining order. The Iraqi security sector, however, disappeared—army conscripts deserted, army officers and police personnel left their posts, and members of the security services went underground.

This wholesale collapse of the security sector was a microcosm of the wider paralysis of Iraqi governance at all levels. The nature of the bureaucratic authority structures in the Saddamite state meant that the removal of the ministers did not simply make room for their subordinates to take over and carry on. Power and authority in the Saddamite system had been too centralized to allow competent subordinates to emerge.

In addition to the top-down paralysis of governance institutions as a result of regime change, the coalition soon discovered that Iraq's administrative, social, and physical infrastructures were in a far worse state than had been expected. A common view among prewar observers, propagated by the Saddam regime, was that Iraq was a relatively modern and developed society. This was certainly true until the early 1990s, when Iraq had boasted a relatively highly educated middle class and extensive access to world markets. However, by 2003 Iraq's governing bureaucracies were hollowed out, its society was impoverished and fractured along lines of clan loyalties, and its physical infrastructure was often held together by the proverbial wire and string. The reality of Iraq's deteriorated and neglected systems meant that reconstruction of social and physical infrastructures was a far more challenging task than had been expected.

The failure to gain UN Security Council support for the invasion of Iraq meant that the coalition was unable to draw on the experience of the international community with post-conflict reconstruction and transition. More concretely, the coalition was unable to draw on tested mechanisms and experienced individuals, either in the UN system or among a wider range of states. The CPA also dealt with a number of rapidly evolving approaches to political transition. These included the creation of the IGC, the appointment of interim ministers, the revitalization of provincial councils, the long-running debate over national elections, and the eventual formation of the Iraqi interim Government in June 2004.

The final surprise was the emergence of a number of insurgent and terrorist campaigns. Although a certain amount of resistance by paramilitary forces had been experienced during the invasion, it was not expected that organized resistance would be a significant challenge to the coalition or the new Iraqi state.

In sum, the prewar planning effort was weakened by both conceptual and organizational errors. Conceptually, the coalition's assumptions about the postwar environment proved overoptimistic about the prospects for a relatively peaceful transfer of authority to new Iraqi governing institutions. Organizationally, the coalition did not prepare its institutions responsible for postwar planning or mission management early enough or integrate them well enough with other government agencies.

Lessons Learned

Design and exercise institutional arrangements before a mission, and develop personnel policies conducive to deploying the most appropriate expertise. Ideally, a mission plan should first start from principles—an understanding of the policy goals and desired end-states, an analysis of the needs of the post-conflict state, and an understanding of the dynamics of the underlying conflict. It should then move on to determining a strategy that makes best use of international resources in a prioritized and sequenced manner to address the critical issues at the right time.

Question assumptions and assessments. The fact that prewar planning assumptions proved to be badly flawed is not a sign of a systemic problem in itself—mistakes happen, and the weakness of the Iraqi state surprised many observers. The systemic problem was that these assumptions could not be effectively challenged in the coalition's political-military planning process.

Integrate planning, decisionmaking authority, and resource allocation and management. These processes were never effectively integrated. This was evident both in Baghdad and in the interagency process.

Ensure that planning. resource allocation, and budgeting processes are integrated in mission and capitals.

Set goals commensurate with the available resources. Divergence between a mission's mandate and its resources is one of the key causes of failure. All too frequently, even when Baghdad made it clear that resources were required to implement the plan, these were not made available by London, Washington, or other capitals.

Build mechanisms that ensure unity of effort in a mission. In the UN system, considerable work is being done on the concept of "integrated missions;" this will be a step in the right direction in the international context.

Build the required institutions before a crisis, and organize and staff them appropriately.

Early planning must be adequate, and mission leadership must build planning and reporting processes into a system that they routinely use for decisionmaking. Mechanisms must be built into planning processes to challenge assumptions and plan for failures, as well as to audit performance. They also need to make appropriate distinctions between the international, country, and local levels of planning and management, while ensuring transparency and feedback up and down the chain of command. The planning process must be integrated with the resource allocation and management process if the mission is to be able to sensibly align priorities with resources.

At the institutional level, leaders of institutions need to take into consideration that:

- Compassion heals. Finding meaning in chaos, openly expressing feelings, being present physically and emotionally, communicating the institution's values—all of these remind people of their work's larger purpose as they grapple with everyday challenges, inspiring action amid agony.

- When organizations cause emotional pain through bad bosses, layoffs, and change, a certain breed of "healing" manager steps in to keep the organization functioning. What to do: listen empathetically, suggest solutions, work behind the scenes to prevent conflict, reframe difficult messages.

- Employees can be helped to find personal fulfillment in ways that advance organizational goals by applying three mutually reinforcing strategies: (1) Clarify what's important and focus on—outcome, not process; (2) Take time to learn about employees' personal situations; this builds trust and helps create opportunities that capitalize on the knowledge that employees bring to the business from outside work; and (3) Continually experiment with how the work gets done—reengineering work processes can improve performance and simplify employees' lives at the same time.

Finally, significant reform requires two factors that do not often come together: a broad-based, popular sentiment that "things have to change," and a leadership that is able to translate this broad dissatisfaction into a concrete program that crystallizes the issues and points to their solution. Most of the time, democratic politics turns out to be quite conservative. Reform is difficult. But, amazingly, reform nonetheless happens.

As I traveled throughout the country visiting and connecting with the more than 250 municipal offices, talking to staff, and meeting and discussing issues of mutual importance and interest with local tribal and religious leaders across the country, it was impossible not to be impressed by the character and drive, the dedication and enthusiasm, the wearied endurance of the men and women in the field, and the enormous opportunities, challenges, and risks before them all.

Essay 4

Preemptive Post-conflict Stabilization and Reconstruction

By Barbara K. Bodine

Any decent surgeon will tell you that all operations are complex; none are simple, routine or risk-free. Any doctor who would say otherwise is ignorant or arrogant and, in either case, potentially lethal. A successful surgical operation requires competent, experienced leadership, strong staff work, training and experience, an understanding of the risks and possible complications, and the necessary back up and a willingness to call it in when the situation warrants. It also begins with a proper diagnosis of the problem. And so it is with complex operations.

There were four major decision points on Iraq: whether to go in, how to go in, what to do the Day After and, in 2006, how to change course significantly to pull Iraq back from the brink of the abyss. This is not the place to debate whether there was good and sufficient cause to invade Iraq in 2003. Most of the rationales and excuses are threadbare by now. The merits of the Rumsfeld Doctrine, "shock and awe" and the size of the force General Franks ultimately had at his disposal, and related issues of martial law all played in the debacle of the Day After, and the need to create (or recreate) counterinsurgency doctrine. These also have been examined in great depth by others.

Much has been made of the revolutionary nature of the new COIN doctrine, often called the Petraeus Doctrine: the maxim that force can lose a counterinsurgency but not win one; the primacy of the political over the military; the centrality of protection of the population over the killing of the enemy; and, the unity-of-effort or whole-of-government

31

approach.[1] What is revolutionary is not that these lessons were new, that they were unique to Iraq, or to 21st century conflict. What is revolutionary was that these lessons had been learned, known, and consciously forgotten—ghosts of conflicts past and lost. What is revolutionary about the COIN doctrine is that it reached into the past, brought it forward, and updated it. It was not the reinvention of the wheel, but a rediscovery that the principles of the wheel still applied. A core element is not the demilitarization of broader counterinsurgency operations, but the de-civilianization of the military. It is a recognition that the complexity of an operation and the broad scope of an operation—interagency, civilian-military, and multilateral—are potential strengths, not inherent weaknesses.

After leaving the State Department, I was fortunate to land as a fellow at the Kennedy School of Government's Institute of Politics. Early on, I gave a lecture entitled "Ad hoc'ing our way to Baghdad," about how our refusal to plan, to draw on the work of the 18-month interagency Future of Iraq Project, to adequately staff (we had about 120 civilians to run a shattered country of 25 million), and our lack of a clear mandate or authority made a mockery of our vaulted political rhetoric. Regime change in Iraq was not a repudiation of President Bush's pledge not to do nation-building but its manifestation.

The Rumsfeldian version of unity of effort through not only unilateral military action, but also uni-agency operations (both covered by fig leafs of coalition partnerships and interagency participation) was seductively simple and streamlined on the surface, but ultimately counterproductive. It forfeited the expertise, legitimacy, and checks and balances of multiple players. Over time, it became insular, isolated, and detached. The costs were evident as Iraq spun out of control and we lacked not only the doctrine and the tools to respond, but also the expertise to properly understand and diagnose the problem.

The working assumption was that we would go in, dust off the Iraqi bureaucracy (which would be in its offices as if on "pause"), patch up the infrastructure, install a government (the famously oxymoronic concept of "imposed democracy"), and be gone by the end of summer. General Jay Garner, the head of the Office of Reconstruction and

---

[1] See Field Manual 3-24 *Counterinsurgency* (Washington, DC: Department of the Army, December 2006), available at <http://www.usgcoin.org/library/doctrine/COIN-FM3-24.pdf>.

Humanitarian Assistance (ORHA), precursor to Paul Bremer's Coalition Provisional Authority (CPA), missed few opportunities to remind his staff of the short tenure of his contract, which turned out to be even shorter than advertised.

To the extent there was a plan, it was drafted in Kuwait (by a British officer), was no more than an inch thick, explicitly was not shared interagency, reflected a grudging acceptance of coalition civilian contributions, had little apparent Iraqi contribution beyond OSD's chosen few, and was not systematically coordinated prior to or after our arrival with the U.S. military. An insurgency may have been inevitable in Iraq, but the size and intensity of the conflagration was not. The Future of Iraq Project, even if fully implemented, was no silver bullet, but to ignore Eisenhower's dictum that the value of a plan is in the planning—and the planners—and to go in without either evidenced a fatal combination of arrogance and idiocy.

Many have asked when we knew we had a train wreck on our hands. It was clear in April 2003 in Baghdad, late March in Kuwait, and even early March in the Pentagon. The Presidential mandate giving DOD the lead on reconstruction of post-invasion Iraq was not bestowed until late January 2003. The Coordinator for Reconstruction for Baghdad and the Central Governorates was not recruited until the end of February 2003, and started on March 2, 2003. There was no staff, no structure, no recruiting process, and no resources. The pretense that ORHA was a civilian organization was perhaps more palatable to the American public, but the effect of the policy was obscure to those within ORHA, ambiguous to the U.S. military, and befuddling to the Iraqis. Donning a suit does not make one civilian anymore than my donning desert cammies made me military. The top ORHA leadership and the coordinators for two of the three regions were retired Army generals. All lacked sustained regional expertise and broad post-conflict credentials, and all evidenced minimum interagency or multilateral experience. The 120 or so civilians in ORHA to manage a shattered country of 25 million were dwarfed by the military and nearly crippled by a leadership culture that denied interagency and coalition experts the communications, transportation, and translation resources necessary to get outside the Green Zone to do our jobs.

This last point was brought home tellingly at the conclusion of my ad-hoc'ery lecture. A young man came up afterwards, a former Army officer and West Point graduate who had been in Baghdad the same time as I. He had been assigned to the Dura neighborhood, later one of the bloodiest districts in the city. He recounted his frustration and anger at the reconstruction tasks he faced, the expectations of the Iraqis in his charge, and the lack of any tools with which to work. How was he to fix the electrical grid, the sewage problem, the water, or any of the other challenges his district faced? Who could he turn to for advice, assistance, or access to city plans? *Were* there any city plans?

The irony is that, as he was coping as best he could at the district level with no guidance, just a mandate to get it done, my small team and I were meeting daily with the mayoralty, the deputy mayors and director generals who ran the city before the invasion and had stayed after liberation to keep it running. Most were dedicated technocrats who had operated under the radar of the Ba'ath Party. In a sense, they were those Iraqi bureaucrats we had counted on to run the city, the ministries, and the country on our behalf. We had access to the officials with the knowledge, the plans, and the experience to fix many of that Army major's problems. The tragedy is that our structure was set up in such a way that neither my team and I nor the Baghdad technocrats had any way of knowing what the major and his neighborhood needed, or any way to get it to him, and he had no way to communicate with us. In fact, until we met in Boston, he did not even know there was an American operation in the city he could turn to. The firewalls between the reconstruction effort and the military effort were impenetrable. The cost to our mission and to the Iraqis is incalculable.

The tectonic shift in approach under the COIN doctrine, the creation of provincial reconstruction teams, the establishment of State's Coordinator for Reconstruction and Stabilization Office (S/CRS), and the Center for Complex Operations make manifest the necessity of thinking through and planning for complex operations, of breaking through that firewall we faced in Iraq in 2003. They leave open the critical question of how to avoid the next Iraq, the Iraq of the Day After. It is not just a question of complex *post*-conflict operations, but complex *pre*-conflict intervention and planning.

What is the lesson we are trying to learn here? How to do the next Iraq better? How to do Afghanistan? Or how not to have to do Iraq or Afghanistan again? If our focus is simply on post-conflict operations, or counterinsurgency, we may consign ourselves to an endless round of low-grade conflicts. The principle threats to our national security, global economic interests, and national values will not come from rival superpowers, but rather from weak, failing, or failed states. Of the countless lessons of 9/11, an important one is that to ignore the remote is to invite disaster. We walked away from post-Soviet Afghanistan and paid the price. We refused to plan for a post-Saddam Iraq and paid a price. And, given the scourge du jour—piracy—we may have ignored Somalia long enough to pay a price. If our lessons learned are how to better respond to a Taliban, an anti-occupation insurgency, or the Barbary Pirates redux, then keep a copy of the FM 3-24 handy and learn its basic lessons well. Internalize whole-of-government and unity-of-effort approaches, protection of the population, the primacy of the political, the centrality of legitimacy, and the requirement for sustainable economic development. Those are good lessons and the right lessons, and if used as touchstones rather than a template, we will do the next Iraq and the next Afghanistan well. (I would strongly encourage we resist the temptation to try this in Somalia.)

Option B to managing the next post-conflict operation well is to take these principles of counterinsurgency and post-conflict stabilization and front load them. This is not a plea for the hoary matrices that seek to predict the next failed state with the same degree of accuracy as predictions of California earthquakes. This is not an endorsement of the concept of responsibility to protect, which has much to recommend it, but also significant drawbacks. But short of an over-quantification of the problem, or an over-internationalization of the response, most decent analysts and practitioners know which states and governments are fraying around the edges but have not yet disintegrated.

I would propose Yemen as an example. Yemen is the always almost failing state. In the late 1970s there was a famous if now forgotten series of cables from the Embassy entitled "Yemen at the Crossroads." Yemen is still at the crossroads. It remains impoverished, with a capacity-deficit governing structure, an illiterate population, inadequate health and medical care, and neighbors who wish it no good. It has had to deal with every flavor of insurgent threat, from Marxist-inspired, to Saudi-funded, to al-Qaeda wannabes, and, *possibly*, Iranian provocateurs. It has no resource base and no exportable commodity of any quantity, other than migrant workers.

What is remarkable is not Yemen's fragility but its durability. It is held together not by rentier largesse or police-state controls. Rather, it sits somewhere between viable if emerging democracy and liberal autocracy. It holds together largely because the Yemenis want it to and see no credible alternative to the current arrangement—the primordial federalism practiced deftly by the central government and the tribal leaders. Centrifugal and centripetal forces act as checks and balances on the power and aspirations of both sides. There is no viable secessionist movement, and neither the regionalism nor the clan structure rise to a level that would presage another Somalia or Iraq, or even the warlordism of Afghanistan. A strong Yemeni identity predates any artificiality of the colonial period and trumps but does not replace tribal/clan identities. Yemenis, like the rest of us, can and do hold multiple identities simultaneously and comfortably.

But not failing is not the same as succeeding. It is as dangerous for us to overvalue subsidiary identities, such as regionalism or clans, as it is to undervalue legitimate grievances of income distribution and corruption, or the willingness of outside players to meddle in the affairs of state. I was in Yemen in January 2009. U.S. policy toward Yemen has become singularly focused, to the point of distortion, on security and counterterrorism, and al-Qaeda specifically. And the dialogue has become increasingly narcissistic—what has Yemen done for us today? How does it support *our* game plan and *our* priorities? The embassy looks like a mini-Green Zone.

No serious Yemeni suggests that al-Qaeda and its followers are not a problem and a legitimate issue for the United States, or that there are not serious security issues in the country that the government needs to address. Their lament is that U.S. policy is focused solely on the short-term and security—the military and the police. The United States is no longer seen as being willing to engage *with* the Yemeni government and to seek to address chronic problems of education, health, development, and, yes, corruption. The Yemenis suggest rebalancing the relationship in terms of a balance between security, development and core diplomacy, and also a balance through a broader dialogue.

What would a policy of preemptive stabilization and reconstruction look like, of playing the lessons of complex operations forward, in a place like Yemen?

Security first becomes security only. In most weak states, the military and the police are very weak links, but an over-reliance on building these two sectors prior to strengthening the broader state capacity can distort the civilian-military balance, send mixed signals on the primacy of civilian control, undermine efforts at governance reform and liberalization, and fail to build the core pillars of the state, including a competent judiciary, not just competent cops. An over-reliance on catching or killing the bad guys without equal commitment to the structures of justice and state services is as hollow and self-defeating as the conflation of democratic processes (elections) with democratic governance.

The military and the police are instruments of state legitimacy, not substitutes for or precursors of the state. State legitimacy is critical to state security but reflects a broader sense of social contract through equitable provision of services, accountability, transparency, and rule of law.

Extension of the authority of the state must be done in parallel with, if not on the heels of, expansion of the legitimacy of the state. This means education, health, rule of law, and structures of trade and commerce. The same investment in teachers, clinic workers and midwives, local judges, and the like as in police and military; the same investment in the building of schools, hospitals, and courts as in police stations and equipment; the same attention to an education *system*, health *system* and judicial *system*. This is not social engineering, or "nation-building" but state capacity-building. This also need not be a U.S.-only endeavor but should be broadly multilateral.

Diplomats and development officers need to get outside the comfort (and confines) of the embassy. We need to understand and work within the realities of pragmatic "risk management" and not cling to the fantasy of "risk avoidance."

The Department of State needs to regain its footing as the coordinator for the formulation and implementation of foreign policy writ large—not just the validation of the Chief of Mission authorities, but recognition that, as a properly functioning NSC staff coordinates the policies of the President and acts as honest broker to the many department and agency stakeholders, both the embassy country team and the Department of State need to get comfortable again with the obligations and responsibilities as policy coordinators in Washington and in the field.

We need to approach failing states, or potentially failing states, with the same unity-of-effort/whole-of-government policies and programs we now recognize are critical for success in failed states and post-conflict environments. We need to recognize it will take the same commitment of time but, if done properly, need not demand the same commitment of resources as we now understand are required for post-conflict operations or for counterinsurgency. While it may be useful to have a corps of professionals and reservists who can deploy quickly to a crisis or post-conflict situation, we must be wary of creating too insular a corps, however interagency it may be. The tools and mindset needed to work complex operations, and the discipline to go when called, should be encouraged, supported, rewarded, and expected throughout the civilian interagency. Creating too narrow a community would let everyone else off the hook.

Essay 5

Lessons Learned in the Fog of Peace

By L. Paul Bremer

After the overthrow of Saddam Hussein, the United Nations designated the Coalition Provisional Authority (CPA) as the government of Iraq. The CPA and Coalition forces faced three major challenges: providing security for the Iraqi people, beginning a process of political reform, and starting to repair the economy. Coalition military forces, under American command, had responsibility for security; the CPA, as the civilian arm of the occupation, had primary responsibility for political and economic reform. In each case, conditions were much worse than prewar planners had anticipated.

Lack of Security

After Saddam's fall, looting caused the widespread destruction of Iraqi government institutions. Some looters were implementing prewar plans of Saddam's security services. Others looted out of anger, revenge, or greed. They roamed the streets at will. The Iraqi army had dissolved itself; not a single Iraqi army unit was intact anywhere in Iraq. Iraqi police had left the streets. Government leaders had vanished. Lacking orders to stop the looting, Coalition forces stood by while the destruction continued. Seventeen of Iraq's 20 government ministries were destroyed. Military barracks and police stations across Iraq were looted and demolished. The country's electrical power and oil infrastructure were badly damaged. The looting cost Iraq more than $12 billion, equivalent to half the country's prewar GDP.

The early failure to maintain order strengthened militias, encouraged insurgents and terrorists, and eroded Iraqi civilian support for Coalition political and economic projects.

Politics Distorted

Saddam Hussein modeled the ruling Baath Party on the Nazi party. The party controlled every aspect of Iraqi life. Competing secret services spied on Iraqis, enlisting children to report on their parents. All information was tightly controlled. Criticism was met by imprisonment, torture, or death. Most non-Baath party political leaders were imprisoned, murdered, or driven into exile. During his 35-year reign, Saddam's regime killed more than one million Iraqis.

At liberation, there was no political structure on which to build a new Iraqi system. Saddam's "constitution" was a constitution only in name. Political parties had been outlawed. Iraq had no laws governing elections and no constituency boundaries. The last reliable census had been taken in 1957. Iraqi exiles, on whom some prewar planners had counted for leadership, were viewed with suspicion by Iraqis who had stayed and suffered under Saddam.

A Shattered Economy

Iraq's economy was already flat on its back in 2003. In 1980, per capita income had been equal to that of Spain; by 2002 it had fallen to that of Angola. During the 1990s, Saddam cut health care spending by over 90 percent. According to the World Bank, in 2002, Iraq had the region's lowest life expectancy and highest infant mortality rates.

The Baath party and its cronies dominated every aspect of the country's economy. Extravagant subsidies ate up half of Iraq's budget. Saddam covered annual fiscal deficits by printing more money. Fridays he would call the Central Bank to order the amount of currency to be printed the next week. The Iraqi Planning Ministry estimated the annual rate of inflation as 115,000 percent at the end of 2002.

Under Saddam, the country produced only 60 percent of needed electricity. Immediately following Saddam's ouster, Iraq was producing only 3 percent of demand. Iraq's state-owned enterprises (SOEs) subsisted on politically determined financing, controlled markets, access to favorable exchange rates, and corruption. Before the war, the Iraqi government estimated unemployment at over 50 percent.

Lack of security after the invasion magnified these structural problems. All of Iraq's banks were closed. There was no system for the electronic transfer of funds; government expenses had to be paid in cash all over the country. Seventy percent of Iraq's hospitals were closed; none of the 22 hospitals in Baghdad had emergency generators. Three thousand schools and 80 percent of their supplies and equipment had been damaged or destroyed. The World Bank estimated that Iraq faced an infrastructure deficit of some $100 billion—four times the country's GDP.

The Coalition confronted the equivalent of a defeated Germany in 1945 and a failed Soviet Union in 1989 combined. Below are several lessons to be learned from the experience of the CPA.

Providing Security for the Civilian Population is Essential to All other Goals.

The fundamental responsibility of any government is to provide security for its citizens. Coalition forces were slow to do this. During the 14-month occupation, attacks tripled. By the end of 2006, as sectarian violence mounted, attacks were seven times higher than they had been in May 2003.

Much remains unclear about America's planning for the post-conflict period. Despite the exceptional bravery and dedication of our armed forces, their efforts were hampered by three problems:

The Coalition did not commit sufficient forces. Public prewar studies and previous planning indicated that to stabilize a country of 27 million people the Coalition would need as many as 500,000 troops; less than half that number was deployed. The initial post-conflict plan called to reduce this force by 80 percent within 3 months of the end of major combat operations. Conditions in Iraq soon overcame this plan; the Coalition never had sufficient "boots on the ground".

America did not plan for or conduct a modern counterinsurgency strategy dedicated to securing the civilian population until 2007. During most of the first year, Coalition forces were based in large forward operating bases outside main cities in hopes of reducing the impression of occupation and rapidly returning security functions to the Iraqis. Coalition forces conducted operations into those cities, but returned to their bases without leaving behind forces to secure the population and support rebuilding the economy. Arguably, in 2003 American forces were not adequately trained or equipped for counterinsurgency operations. Despite increasing improvements in these capabilities, the Coalition proved slow in adapting to the growing violence and insurgency in Iraq.

American armed forces were hampered by restrictive rules of engagement. They did not have authority to stop the postwar looting. Only when conditions worsened and the full extent of the lawlessness was understood by senior leaders did ROEs change. Some Coalition allies' troops operated under ROEs that even prevented them from coming to the aid of American forces and civilians under attack.

The Coalition understood that Iraq's security eventually had to be the responsibility of Iraqi forces. But early efforts to train a professional army and police force were ill-planned and under-resourced. A proposal, supported by Coalition military and political leaders in Iraq, for the U.S. Army to train the new Iraqi army was disapproved in Washington, this being perceived as a civil governance function better suited to non-military agencies and organizations. America lacked the capacity to create a professional police force on a national scale, especially when the police were simultaneously engaged in counterinsurgency operations. The transition to a more effective, adequately resourced, civilian-military police strategy took more than 3 years.

The CPA's decision to "disband" the Iraqi army has been much commented upon. The decision recognized practical and political realities. By the fall of Baghdad in April, Iraq's army had already "self-demobilized", as DOD put it. The question for the Coalition was whether to recall Saddam's army. Practical and political factors argued against that course. Saddam's had been a conscript army, the majority of whose enlisted men were Shias serving under often-brutal Sunni officers. When the army dissolved itself, those enlisted men went back to their homes or farms. To reconstitute the army, Coalition military would have had to find the draftees and force them back into service. Moreover, there would be no place to put the recalled forces, because postwar looting had destroyed all military barracks and facilities—sometimes leaving not one brick standing on another.

Political arguments against recalling the army were decisive. While Iraq's army had once been an honorable institution, it had recently served as an instrument of Saddam's tyranny. It had conducted a decade-long war against the Kurds, killing hundreds of thousands of them, and forcing still more out of their homes. The army had been used to suppress the Shia after the first Gulf War, indiscriminately killing hundreds of thousands of men, women, and children. Between them, the Kurds and Shia represent 80 percent of Iraq's population, and their leaders made clear to the CPA that they strongly disapproved of recalling Saddam's army. Kurdish leaders even threatened to secede from Iraq.

So instead the Coalition trained and built a new, all-volunteer army. The Coalition paid severances to all former enlisted men, and pensions to all but the top officers from Saddam's army. Enlisted men and officers up to colonel from the former army were encouraged to apply for the new institution after proper vetting. By the time the occupation ended, over 80 percent of the enlisted men in the new army and almost all the NCOS and officers were from the former army. The decision to build a new army has proven a correct one. Today, the new Iraqi army is the country's most respected security institution. By contrast, the Iraqi police, whom the CPA did recall to duty, continue to be plagued by accusations of corruption and brutality.

Coalition intelligence was slow to focus on the growing threat of terrorists and insurgents. For the first 6 months, at the direction of Washington, U.S. intelligence focused on the search for WMD. Intelligence experts in counterterrorism and counterinsurgency did not arrive in any numbers until late 2003.

Some of these problems were due to unrealistic prewar planning assumptions concerning the security situation in the post-conflict period, which postulated a functioning Iraqi government and security force after the end of combat operations. No prewar plan can anticipate all possible scenarios; plans must be flexible to account for realities on the ground. But little worst-case planning appears to have been done.

Insecurity opened the door for al-Qaeda's vicious strategy of killing Iraqi civilians, particularly Shia, as well as for sectarian violence, crime, and growing unrest at the perceived Coalition occupation. Finding themselves under attack, with neither the Coalition nor nascent Iraqi security forces able to protect them, many Iraqis turned to local militia or supported insurgent and criminal groups, who came to dominate many of the neighborhoods, towns, and villages. After the CPA left Iraq, this led to a vicious spiral of violence and sectarian killing.

Political Progress Requires Active but Flexible Engagement

Most post-conflict societies have experienced brutal rule. Iraq was no exception. Its political culture was fragile. Repairing it would require Iraq's communities to make concessions. In theory, it might have been preferable for the Coalition to take a hands-off approach, letting the Iraqis sort out their political future. But distrust, fear, and the lack of security made it difficult for Iraqi leaders to take responsibility on their own. Active and flexible Coalition engagement was essential, with the Coalition playing a balancing role between the various Iraqi communities.

In his April 10, 2003, "Freedom Message", CENTCOM commander, General Tommy Franks outlawed the Baath Party. This action was consistent with prewar plans and with recommendations from Iraqi political groups in exile before the war. A CPA order in May specified that members of the top one percent of the Baath Party, the hard core of Saddam's regime, would no longer be allowed to have government jobs. They were, however, free to find work in the burgeoning private sector, become journalists or farmers, or retire in peace. This was a correct and popular decision. However, as leader of the CPA, I mistakenly turned its implementation over to Iraqi politicians, who sought to significantly broaden the scope of the CPA's narrowly drawn policy. It would have been wiser to give this responsibility to a select group of Iraqi jurists.

The CPA found it important to establish a clear process with firm deadlines for Iraq's political reconstruction. But the plan had to adjust to realities. The CPA initially proposed that Iraqi leaders convene a constitutional convention to draft a modern constitution. When it became clear that the Iraqis would not take that step, the CPA encouraged Iraqis to draft an interim constitution. Only then did Iraqi factions begin serious negotiations, with the CPA playing a vigorous, behind-the-scenes role to help build consensus on key issues. This Interim Constitution became the basis for the National Constitution approved by the Iraqi people in 2005.

CPA plans to establish an elected Iraqi government were altered by realities. Conventional wisdom concerning post-conflict countries recommends avoiding early elections because they tend to favor the best organized and often most sectarian communities. CPA and UN election experts understood the danger of holding elections only 6 months after the occupation ended, but the Shia community and its leaders, comprising over 60 percent of the population, insisted on early elections as the price for their support of the new constitution. Ignoring their demand would have led to a collapse of the entire political process.

Unsurprisingly, sectarian and ethnic tensions persist; they will take time to overcome. But the CPA's vigorous engagement in political reconstruction gave Iraqis the opportunity to shape their country's democratic future, based on one of the region's most progressive constitutions.

Post-Conflict Economies Require Immediate Stimulus and Fundamental Reform

The immediate priority is to stimulate economic activity and restore essential services. Decades of bureaucratic caution meant that Iraqi civil servants lacked the habit of initiative, so a vigorous but flexible Coalition role was essential. Millions of Iraqi civil servants and pensioners had not been paid for months; the CPA paid them within days, raising pensions ten-fold. Salaries for doctors were raised eight-fold, and for teachers 50-fold. Import duties were waived. After these measures, economic activity immediately blossomed in all major cities.

Within 3 months of assuming its role, the CPA reopened all Iraq's banks, hospitals, public clinics, and schools. More than 1,000 schools had been rebuilt. Electricity and oil production had returned to prewar levels where, despite daily attacks by terrorists and insurgents, they remained until the CPA departed.

The long-term health of a post-conflict economy depends on laying the foundations of a modern economy by implementing responsible monetary and fiscal policies. The CPA established the independence of the Central Bank and freed interest rates to be determined by the market, not bureaucrats. Working with Iraqi ministers, the CPA produced balanced budgets for 2003 and 2004.

Iraq's currency was worthless, so the CPA replaced Iraq's entire currency. This operation meant importing over 6,000 tons of new currency—enough to fill 30 747 aircraft—and distributing it through hundreds of exchange stations throughout Iraq. The process was completed without incident in the midst of widespread violence and insurgency.

As with its political program, realities on the ground forced adjustments in the CPA's economic plans. For political and social reasons, the CPA was unable to reduce the huge, Saddam-era food and energy subsidies distorting Iraq's budget. While the economic arguments for cutting them were clear, Iraqi political arguments against the reductions, influenced by the increasing violence, were decisive. Similarly, the CPA's program to reform the SOEs was deferred in favor of keeping hundreds of thousands of employees on a payroll throughout the occupation, even when the businesses were shuttered.

Despite these setbacks, CPA economic policies bore significant fruit. By June 2004, when the occupation ended, Iraq's economy was recovering. Oil and electricity production were at or above prewar levels, despite constant attacks on Iraqi infrastructure. The banking system was rebounding. Inflation had been reduced to about two percent. According to the United Nations Development Programme, unemployment had fallen to ten percent. The International Monetary Fund estimated that Iraq's economy grew almost 44 percent in 2004.

The Coalition's vigorous economic actions did not solve Iraq's problems. After the CPA left, the erosion of security undermined progress. Iraq's economy is still riven by corruption and distorted by its over-dependence on a state-controlled commodity base. But the elements of sound economics were put in place and should serve the Iraqi people well as security improves.

Mobilizing for Nation-Building

A final lesson is the need for the entire U.S. Government to be fully engaged in planning, preparing for, and supporting post-conflict efforts. This did not happen in Iraq, partly because of flawed prewar planning and a failure of the interagency coordination process. Even after it became clear that Iraq was in worse shape than expected, the U.S. Government was not structured to support the effort demanded by the realities on the ground.

Successful post-conflict efforts require that personnel, programs, policies, and procedures be in place beforehand. These must draw on capabilities in the private sector, too. Fortunately the Executive Branch and Congress have recognized this need and begun to fund it.

Essay 6

Complex Operations in Practice

By Peter W. Chiarelli

The U.S. experiences in Iraq and Afghanistan underscore the complexity of modern conflict and the lack of U.S. Government organizational constructs that can effectively deal with this complexity. Despite some useful adjustments since 2001, the U.S. Government fundamentally remains organized for an era of bipolar containment and deterrence rather than the challenges of stabilizing failed and failing states. The multi-dimensional challenges of modern conflicts have resulted in ad hoc orchestrations of all the instruments of national power that are not in tune with the strategic context.

As the commander of the 1st Cavalry Division in Baghdad during Operation *Iraqi Freedom II* (OIF II), and subsequently as the commander of Multi-National Corps-Iraq in 2006, I learned that managing the interwoven kinetic and non-kinetic complexity of modern conflict, not only within the host nation, but within the joint, interagency, and international environments, is the defining characteristic—therefore the challenge—of future operations.

The only national security instrument organizationally designed to operate in complex environments—the military, with its numbers and resources—swamps the capabilities of other, often more appropriate agencies designed for the non-kinetic aspects of complex environments. Short of full-scale overhaul of the U.S. Government, how can we create the capacity to manage and dominate these environments while our national security functions catch up to the speed and flexibility needed in an information age security environment? Part of the answer is to make adjustments to our military forces so they can respond to a greater range of challenges. The Army has taken some major steps in this direction. The other part of the answer is to get our strategy right, being able to identify, understand, and rapidly adjust ways and means to achieve strategic objectives to events on the ground.

A Full Spectrum Army

The Army concept of full spectrum operations[1] recognizes that we must work in tandem with joint, interagency, and international stakeholders to balance the application of all the instruments of national power. It assumes that purely kinetic operations are no longer the norm, and in most cases the decisive elements in complex operations are more likely to be non-kinetic and informational than kinetic. It fully recognizes Sir Rupert Smith's dictum:

> War amongst the people is different: it is the reality in which the people in the streets and houses and fields—all the people, anywhere—are the battlefield. Military engagements can take place anywhere: in the presence of civilians, against civilians, in defence of civilians. Civilians are the targets, objectives to be won, as much as an opposing force.[2]

The Army recently published a field manual on stability operations, FM 3-07.[3] Written with the assistance and collaboration of multiple government and nongovernmental organizations, it provides a framework within which Army forces can work in concert with other agencies and interested stakeholders. FM 3-07 prescribes a level of coordination that will facilitate more rapid movement from concept to action to results.

---

[1] "The Army's operational concept: Army forces combine offensive, defensive, and stability or civil support operations simultaneously as part of an interdependent joint force to seize, retain, and exploit the initiative, accepting prudent risk to create opportunities to achieve decisive results. They employ synchronized action—lethal and nonlethal—proportional to the mission and informed by a thorough understanding of all variables of the operational environment. Mission command that conveys intent and an appreciation of all aspects of the situation guides the adaptive use of Army forces." FM 3-0, *Full Spectrum Operations*.

[2] Rupert Smith, *The Utility of Force, The Art of War in the Modern World* (New York: Penguin Books, 2005), 3.

[3] Field Manual 3-07, *Stability Operations* (Washington, DC: Department of the Army, October 2008), available at <http://usacac.army mil/cac2/repository/FM307/FM3-07.pdf>.

The Army has also moved away from an organizational model based on large divisions to a much more flexible, brigade-centric structure. This new approach allows the Army to provide a versatile mix of "tailorable" organizations operating on a predictable, rotational cycle to provide a sustained flow of trained and ready forces for full spectrum operations and at the same time hedge against unexpected contingencies at a rate sustainable for our all-volunteer force.

Operational and Strategic Flexibility

FM 3-07 captures many of the difficult civil-military lessons I learned as the operational commander in charge of day-to-day operations in Iraq in 2006. This transitional period was complicated by a political stalemate and an internally and externally fueled sectarian conflict. Sunni and Shia extremist groups were waging not only a counter-government campaign, but also a broader, ethno-sectarian struggle for power in the country. Once the Government of Iraq (GOI) was seated in late May 2006, the level of sectarian chaos that ensued stunted the political and economic progress that had been achieved in 2004 and 2005.

It was difficult for many to see the Iraqi government as anything more than an agent of a Shia conspiracy rather than the hoped for unity government. The operational themes, or lines of effort, were no longer balanced to support the desired outcome; a pronounced adjustment was identified but did not materialize. The design of the operation needed to adjust to the shifting context.

As an enduring lesson for the execution of complex operations, I would submit that not only recognizing transitions, but changing the campaign design in light of changing realities is fundamental to success. This requires structure and leaders who can create and exercise strategic flexibility, even in the face of seemingly insurmountable bureaucratic inertia.

Shared Objectives

Though we approached the GOI strategically as though it were a monolithic rational actor, it was clear there were diverse organizational dynamics complicated by historical sectarian precedent and contemporary politics. During division operations, and later as the Multi-National Corps-Iraq commander, I learned the importance of cultural awareness to force protection. We intuitively recognized the tactical importance of understanding culture and enforced the strategy through training and re-training.

Understanding the basics of culture is not the same thing as sharing objectives with the host-nation government. While the United States saw the escalating violence in Baghdad in 2006 as a crisis requiring immediate action, the Iraqis did not always share our sense of alarm. It seemed the Iraqis were going through a massive, societal convulsion as they worked through their differences. As the body count in Baghdad continued to rise, I confronted senior Iraqi leaders in an effort to push for a coordinated Coalition-GOI solution. Our differing perceptions became clear in their response: "What's the problem? It was worse under Saddam." The cultural disconnect created a mismatch between Coalition and GOI visions for the country. This disconnect had major tactical, operational, and strategic consequences.

Fighting the Mission, not the Plan

According to FM 3-07, unified action is "the synchronization, coordination, and/or integration of the activities of governmental and nongovernmental entities with military operations to achieve unity of effort."[4] From a Coalition and interagency perspective, clearly working to define operational objectives at an interagency as well as the joint Coalition Force/GOI level ensures a unified operational approach. An important corollary is to continuously fold into the design the strategic value of tactical actions. When actions on the ground significantly alter the construct of the campaign, it is time to reevaluate the ways and means.

The actions of Multi-National Force-West in the Al Anbar region in leveraging a shift of alliances of key informal governance (tribal) powerbrokers at the same time the GOI was struggling to establish legitimacy and capacity revealed a strategic opportunity that could have been leveraged earlier. A unified approach cannot become so rigid that parties become slaves to their plan. The approach must adapt as the actions and results on the ground reveal tactical opportunities that have strategic value.

---

[4] FM 3-07, 1–3.

At the same time, the collaborative approach to unified action needs to optimize and leverage the strengths each partner brings to the operation and the impact it could have on a joint-campaign plan.

As the Task Force for Business and Stability Operations, under Paul Brinkley, worked diligently to reopen many of Iraq's 162 SOEs, resistance began to emerge in an operational context, where development, diplomacy, and defense were pragmatically linked. Ideology replaced pragmatism along a critical line of effort focused on the Iraqi economy. Incorporating different contextual lessons from Eastern Europe, some could not see the impact of employment on the force protection of our servicemen and women and the direct impact creation of jobs would have in marginalizing extremist elements. Opening even a third of the Iraqi SOEs represented a boost in employment, which, as demonstrated in OIF II, has a direct and visible impact on extremist platforms. Yet, at the national level, there was little understanding of complex operations past the establishment of security.

Keeping it Real

The hybrid nature of modern wars demands that we address information as a domain of the global environment. As we waited for the Iraqi government to define itself through the first half of 2006, we simultaneously engaged in an intense information campaign targeting the Iraqi populace in an effort to marginalize extremists and enhance the legitimacy and capacity of the incoming "unification" government. Transplanting a Western concept, we developed many suggestions for tasks that the GOI could accomplish in its first 100 days. An expectation began to emerge of great things to come.

But we failed to understand that the Iraqis had other priorities. For those involved in complex operations over extended periods, the lesson is, don't become too enamored of your own message. The expectations we created in the process impacted the expectations not only of the populace, but also the Coalition. We created our own perception of capacity in a situation where capacity was almost nonexistent, and the organizational dynamics of diverse GOI entities—both legitimate and illegitimate—did not fit the expectations created in the information campaign.

In many ways we repeated the mistakes of past wars. Robert Komer's 1972 DARPA report on the organizational dynamics and institutional constraints in the U.S. approach to the Government of Vietnam is eerily prescient. Replace "GVN" with "GOI" and "Vietnamese" with "Iraqi" and you get a sense for how our own optimism may have impacted our approach:

> The sheer incapacity of the regimes we backed, which largely frittered away the enormous resources we gave them, may well have been the greatest single constraint on our ability to achieve the aims we set ourselves at acceptable cost … for many reasons we did not use vigorously the leverage over the Vietnamese leaders that our contributions gave us. We became their prisoners rather than they ours; the GVN used its weakness far more effectively as leverage on us than we used our strength to lever it.[5]

Our intense desire for the GOI to succeed blinded us to the facts on the ground. We failed to leverage the control we had over ministry and national level capacity and legitimacy because of an optimistic belief created by ourselves that unification across the sects and a rational-actor approach to governance would emerge. Our own doctrine now incorporates this lesson in stark language: "Stability operations leverage the coercive and constructive capabilities of the military force."[6]

The Value of Values

The U.S. military is an incredible learning organization. No other government organization I know can so fundamentally change its approach to how it does business with such efficiency and effectiveness as the U.S. Military. Yet the force during 2006 was uneven in understanding the complexities of counterinsurgency and stability operations. We had not yet completed the cognitive transformation to full spectrum operations and Rupert Smith's understanding of how integral the populace was to creating progress.

It is important to note that, as the complexity of operations rises over extended periods, the challenges to ethical and moral decision-making increase. Exposure to brutal acts grinds on the fundamental belief

---

[5] Robert W. Komer, *Bureaucracy Does Its Thing: Institutional Constraints on U.S.-GVN Performance in Vietnam,* RAND Report R-967-ARPA, August 1972, iv, available at <http://www.rand.org/pubs/reports/2005/R967.pdf>
[6] FM 3-07, 2–2.

systems of our servicemen and women. The clarity of a "just cause" in the grey area between peace and war becomes questioned in the mind of even the strongest. Balancing the cultural understanding needed in complex operations, the impact our culture can have on a host nation, and the horrific acts that are witnessed requires leader attention and consistent "retraining" of the value sets that define our Nation. When the espoused values of the profession of arms are tested by the brutality of extended operations in the harshness of a culturally foreign place like Iraq, the emerging actual values must be addressed. As Abu Ghraib and other incidents have clearly demonstrated, slips in our value set, no matter how "grey" the operating environment may become, can have clear strategic consequences.

Conclusion

Sir Rupert Smith gives us a view into the future of conflict, while Robert Komer starkly reminds us that, "we have been here before." As the fundamental nature of how we define war changes—where linearity is replaced by the interplay of intertwined operational themes, and the populace becomes the battlefield—complexity will rise exponentially.

The balance between lines of effort must be backstopped by cultural understanding, interagency cooperation, unified action, an acknowledgement of our values within the operational context, and flexibility of operational design. If we are to exist and dominate the current and near-term strategic environment, we must address the nature of warfare with a singular focus across the instruments of national power.

What we learned from history we are relearning in Iraq and Afghanistan:

> Lack of any overall management structure contributed to [the strategy's] over-militarization ... the absence of a single agency or directing body charged with [counterinsurgency or pacification] contributed greatly to the prolonged failure to carry it out on any commensurate scale.[7]

The complexity of modern wars and the inability to create a government-level, unified, security apparatus for the contemporary strategic environment forced an ad hoc interagency approach and a

---

[7] Komer, ix.

personality-driven strategic realignment in early 2007 that was, in fact, quite successful.

However, without true understanding of the essence of decision, how bureaucracies create their own inertia, the complexity of modern wars, and the importance of unified efforts, we risk repeating ourselves as we continue forward into an era of persistent commitment.

Essay 7

No Formulas: Bosnia, Haiti, and Kosovo

By Wesley Clark

The history of the military art is replete with examples proving that military power used alone has been ineffective. In fact, outside of limited operations—for example, a hostage rescue—it is rare that a single arm of the service, such as airpower, or even a combined military force would be sufficient to achieve a desired outcome. Even World War II, in which we demanded unconditional surrender and occupied the territories of our defeated adversaries, entailed complicated diplomacy, as well as unusual sacrifices on the home front.

Nevertheless, the enormous destructiveness of modern weaponry, enabled by precision strike, advanced reconnaissance, surveillance, and target acquisition (RSTA), and special operations, fueled by a military establishment working to instill a "warrior spirit" in an all-volunteer force, combined after the Gulf War to mislead many into believing that the "shock and awe" of a modern military strike could in itself produce victory against serious adversaries. And this occurred even as it was becoming apparent that military proficiency was just one component of any larger national security operation.

Many of us thought we'd learned this already, in Vietnam. But it has taken the post-invasion difficulties of Iraq and the struggling, under-resourced mission in Afghanistan to create a new interest in complex operations.

Think of complex operations as those whose requirements extend beyond the traditional air, land, sea, and space forces of the organized military to encompass integrated diplomacy, political and economic development, and intelligence operations. During the 1990s, we had some experience with all these. In 1994, we occupied Haiti to restore the elected President to power. In 1995, we executed an integrated diplomatic-military strategy to end the fighting in Bosnia with the Dayton peace agreement. And NATO's 1999 air campaign to end Serb ethnic cleansing in Kosovo saved a million and a half Albanians from that fate and culminated in a NATO occupation and, ultimately, an independent state. All three offer critical lessons.

Take Haiti first. The "enemy" consisted of 1,400 members of the *Forces Armées d'Haiti*, (FAdH), supporting the ruling junta. Their equipment consisted of just five V-150 armored cars. Our initial plan was for an invasion. The operation had no exit strategy, no diplomatic component, and little interagency support. Over a period of about 10 weeks, we retooled the plan, secured an authorizing UN resolution, created a UN-led force commanded by an American to which we could hand over the operation, and pulled together an interagency working group to consider how to handle Haiti's real problems: crime, poverty, disease, and lack of infrastructure. In the process, we issued the first interagency OPLAN and conducted a full interagency rehearsal.

Still, the results were meager. President Clinton sent a team of "eminences" to talk the junta into surrendering—which they did once they learned that a brigade of the 82nd Airborne Division was en route. The 10th Mountain Division landed without resistance, and President Aristide was reinstalled in his palace. It soon turned out that U.S. forces had to deputize the corrupt FAdH to do the police work. Army reserve lawyers were sent in to try to cope with the Haitian justice system. The prisons were abysmal. The Department of Commerce couldn't win over U.S. investors. Department of Justice police training was fundamentally flawed in its emphasis on "beat cops" instead of what was needed—leaders. The infrastructure programs were under-resourced and inappropriate.

After 6 months, we turned the mission over to the UN. In 2004, the UN had to intervene all over again, because, as one international police trainer told me in 2005, "you boys failed." Still, we learned some lessons. We wrote Presidential Decision Directive 56 to formalize interagency efforts. While, we improved our police training, we did not fix our woeful capabilities to project good government abroad through public health, education, a legal system, anti-corruption, infrastructure investment, and business development. These would have required legislative changes, adjustments in Congressional oversight, and above all, resources that just weren't available.

Bosnia was a little different. Three sides were locked in bitter conflict that had cost perhaps 150,000 lives and made millions homeless. A feckless UN mission was on the ground, hopelessly outmaneuvered diplomatically, as well as out-gunned by at least one side. Several peace efforts, including a 1994 U.S.-led effort, had failed.

We used a revitalized Croatian military force, complemented by a simultaneous NATO air retaliation to brush aside resistance from the strongest side, the Serbs, and compel them to accede to a new peace initiative followed by occupation by more than 30,000 NATO troops. We paid special attention to police forces and the judiciary and applied other obvious lessons from Haiti when we crafted the agreement. We also learned from the failed UN mission in Haiti to get legal authority for the military to take any necessary actions, but refrain from making them responsible for much more than enforcing a ceasefire and cessation of hostilities.

The operation brought an end to the fighting. With much angst, NATO eventually began to detain indicted war criminal suspects. Numerous elections were held. But, some 14 years later, refugee resettlement has clearly failed, political reconciliation has largely failed, and economic redevelopment has stalled. U.S. forces are no longer present on the ground.

Kosovo is a third example of complex operations. More than a decade of colonial-style repression in the region known as Kosovo had thoroughly angered and alienated the ethnic Albanian majority. Minor acts of resistance were met with fierce, violent repression. Efforts to mediate the struggle, leveraged by a NATO air threat, failed. As the slide into conflict with Serbia became inevitable in the early weeks of 1999, the U.S. chain of command seemed exclusively focused on the proposed bombing campaign, and especially target selection. We hadn't spent years developing the target base for Serbia, but we did have more than 8 months to work these targets. In the days leading up to the conflict, we had perhaps 200 targets, and these seemed to mesmerize the top political and military in the U.S. chain of command. On a trip back to the Pentagon, I was alarmed at the extent to which these top leaders had lost sight of the vulnerability of NATO forces in neighboring Macedonia, the fragility of the government there, and how little consideration had been given to defining success in the operation and what it might take to get there. Washington seemed to be indulging in wishful thinking that dropping a few bombs would break the Serbs' will. Experience shows this seldom happens. If Washington had understood that the campaign would take 78 days, 1,000 aircraft, and the threat of a ground invasion, perhaps we would have lost the political will to initiate the operation, and allowed another deeper regional conflict to develop.

It took NATO a week to reach a consensus on our political objectives—what we sought from the Serbs. Fortunately, in the failed, pre-conflict negotiations, we had already created a plan for the post-conflict occupation, but we actually began the operation without hard and fast political objectives. Had we pushed harder earlier to define the objective, we might, in order to maintain allied consensus, have aimed too low. It took a week of Serb intransigence before nations were willing to agree that all Serb forces should leave Kosovo, and that a NATO force should move in.

Two weeks into the operation, after some 15 nights of successful strikes, I met with Secretary of State Madeleine Albright in Brussels. "Well, it's up to you and the bombing," she said. But it wasn't. The outcome of our meeting was an effort to create a diplomatic out for the Serb leader, President Slobodan Milosevic, which culminated in a joint mission headed by Finnish President Maarti Ahtisaari and Russian Vice Premier Viktor Chernomyrdin. They eventually persuaded Milosevic to accept the inevitable.

Milosevic would never have conceded had he had a realistic alternative. It was our job in the military to deprive him of any alternative. We did this by escalating the pressures from the strategic bombing inside Serbia, striking more targets and more sensitive targets, and employing more aircraft and continuous strikes. I asked for things I did not get, like Army Tactical Missile System (ATACMS) strikes and the use of the Apache helicopters. But this kept up the drumbeat of escalation.

We also attempted to ratchet up the effectiveness of the tactical strikes against Milosevic's army and police in Kosovo, a total of perhaps 60,000 mostly mechanized forces. We increased unmanned aerial vehicle (UAV) coverage, used B-52s in area strikes, and deployed Special Forces to the borders. Although it was denied at the time—and I was kept out of the know—it's possible that a combined U.S.-UK intelligence effort was arming the Kosovo Liberation Army in an effort to put a friendly force on the ground against the Serbs inside Kosovo. Somehow, they did get weapons, and they did advance into Kosovo against Serb resistance.

Finally, we began a planning effort that could culminate in early autumn in a six-division, U.S.-led NATO invasion of Kosovo through Albania and Macedonia. And we made sure the Russians knew this so that Milosevic would be in no doubt about what was coming.

In the midst of the conflict, Milosevic was indicted for war crimes by the International Criminal Tribunal for Yugoslavia. He had become an outlaw, which blocked his ability to squirm diplomatically away from NATO's grip.

It was the inevitability of defeat that finally crushed Milosevic. The NATO strikes began in a restrained manner, and NATO nations quaked and quavered under the domestic political backlash of the inevitable accidents and collateral damage of the strikes. But NATO held together. Nothing was more important than this.

In addition, the insurgency blossoming inside Kosovo was on our side, and bitterly opposed to the Serbs. It could only get stronger the longer the Serbs continued their repression and ethnic cleansing.

As the commander of NATO forces, I was in a unique position. working two parallel chains of command—one through the NATO Military Committee to the NATO Secretary General, the other through the Chairman of the Joint Chiefs to the Secretary of Defense and the President. I also had spent hundreds of hours with Milosevic in a relationship dating back almost 4 years to the Dayton peace process for Bosnia. I made my recommendations with a full understanding of the Serb leader. I knew he understood military operations, because he was a graduate of the Serb's Command and Staff College. He also was a trained lawyer who spoke English and understood it perfectly. I knew he was fundamentally rational, and would at some point give in and try to salvage what he could, rather than resist to the bitter end. Few commanders in history have had a better insight into the mind of the opposing leader.

In Kosovo, we bent the laws of war to suit the "laws of politics," helping fearful democracies to move forward to take successful military action. We did not use mass or surprise. Instead, we gave plenty of warning and used air attacks piecemeal. In politics, force is used only as a last resort, after warnings, and then using the absolute minimum of force.

One element we did get right—and its contribution is fundamental—is legal authority. Missions must be legitimate, not just in U.S. law, but, more importantly, in the law of the land in which we are at work. Authorizing UN resolutions, as detailed as possible, are essential.

The weaknesses in complex operations that we never fixed were in interagency support, and those weaknesses have continued to plague U.S. operations in Iraq and Afghanistan. Nation-building remains a dirty word, and yet the success of our operations often depends on it. But where are the contingency budgets, reserve personnel, and trained and willing experts in the fields of public health, agriculture, business development, accounting, police and law enforcement, public affairs, youth activity, family counseling, and dozens of other disciplines that we desperately need? How is it that every provincial reconstruction team in Iraq doesn't have a youth activities leader, doctors who can work public health, a microcredit bureau that establishes banks and microlending, and agricultural representatives with direct access to experimental farms and the seed developers who could revolutionize agricultural productivity? Where are the legions of trained anthropologists and native-fluent scholar-linguists who will dedicate a couple of years to promoting economic and political developments at the local level?

Today, above all looms the problem of Pakistan, where a democratic government's own military institutions have sown the seeds of internal conflict. Surely, this situation requires the most artful blend of diplomacy and discreet assistance in the military, economic, and political development areas.

Now is the time to seek the deeper reforms and more robust resourcing we missed in 1994. But to do so we also need to move beyond the Quadrennial Defense Review as the Nation's principle strategic planning document. It was never meant for that. Where is the real interagency plan for the United States in foreign affairs and national security? Who should be responsible for writing it and tying it to resources? And how do we create and sustain the tens of thousands of trained non-military professionals we need as a nation to succeed in complex operations?

The foundations of complex operations remain tactical and technical proficiency in the military art. Forces must "move, shoot, and communicate." Losses must be avoided and collateral damage minimized. Missions must be defined and rules of engagement formulated. But there are no formulaic solutions. Each situation is different, each challenge unique. And we must be wary that in learning the lessons of past operations we haven't blinded ourselves to the emerging challenges of the future.

The Balkans Revisited: Kosovo 1999

By Timothy Cross

Over the years I have served on UK operations in Northern Ireland, with the UN in Cyprus, with Coalition Forces in the Gulf, and with NATO forces in Bosnia. However, Operation Agricola, the deployment to Kosovo in 1999, was the first time that I came face to face with a large-scale humanitarian crisis. It was a challenging and demanding deployment for me, professionally and personally, but it was nonetheless "simply" another in a series of operations where UK Armed Forces have been faced with humanitarian action. Armed conflict in Rwanda, Angola, East Timor, and Sierra Leone, natural disasters in Mozambique and elsewhere—all created widespread human suffering. On the evidence of recent years, such deployments are on the increase. Amongst many challenges that they bring with them is working alongside, and indeed for, large numbers of non-military agencies. These can be international, like the UNHCR and WFP, governmental, like the UK Department for International Development (DFID), or NGOs, like the ICRC, the Oxford Committee for Famine Relief (OXFAM), and Médecins Sans Frontières (MSF), and the reality of intrastate conflict and natural disasters is that such organizations are present in large numbers; they bring real strengths to bear, and they are key players in bringing relief to those who suffer. A key lesson for me from this deployment was that we, the military, needed to learn more about these agencies, about how they operate and how we can work better with them.

I was appointed to what was to become the 101 Logistic Brigade earlier in this tour, and it was in this capacity that I found myself preparing to go back to the Balkans in late January 1999. The initial intent was to support and help implement an imminent peace agreement that was, at the time, being negotiated at Rambouillet, France. Our aim was to move out from the UK by sea into Greece, entering through the port of Thessalonica. There we would receive the totality of the UK contribution to the NATO-led KFOR and stage it through to Macedonia by road and rail. It would then be integrated, and some in-theater training would be conducted before we moved on up into Kosovo to conduct some form of peace support operation.

This is all referred to as the reception, staging, onward movement, and integration process (RSOI), and, although it had always produced surprises and unexpected developments in previous deployments, events this time were to really overtake us. By mid-February, elements of my brigade were settling into Thessalonica and a number of locations around Skopje, the capital of Macedonia, and we had begun the process of bringing in 4 Armoured Brigade—the bulk of the initial UK combat power. As the armoured vehicles of the first battle group were being offloaded in Thessalonica, the talks began to falter. By the end of February, we had received over 2,000 military personnel and several hundred vehicles into theatre, but the situation was deteriorating quickly, and we realized that the operation was not going to be anything like as straightforward as we had originally thought. While ships and aircraft continued to flow into theatre, the Rambouillet talks soon completely broke down, and NATO commenced the bombing of Belgrade. Early reports began to indicate that the fighting inside Kosovo was escalating, and by mid-March over 200,000 internally displaced persons (IDPs) were reportedly on the move, with several tens of thousand of people crossing Kosovo's international borders into northern Albania and Macedonia. The refugee flows had started in earnest, and the bombing served only to exacerbate matters.

In the port itself we quickly faced riots as the Greek people played out their opposition to the NATO bombing, and local opinion polls showed an overwhelming majority against our presence. The rioters presumably hoped to keep us blockaded in the port. While they failed in that intent, several of our rail convoys were ambushed on their way up to Macedonia, and quite a few of our vehicles were damaged. I had established my brigade headquarters in a hotel complex south of the Macedonian capital, Skopje, and with my staff began to produce a raft of contingency plans for what we thought might emerge. It was abundantly clear to me that the refugee crisis would get worse, so we produced a number of ideas; as usual, of the three options we planned for it was the fourth that actually happened but—and this was perhaps my first key lesson—*commanders and their staffs must not only make military contingency plans, but they must be capable of adapting themselves quickly to non-military requirements as events unfold.*

On Thursday 1st April, I drove out to look at several sites that the Macedonian Government was intending to develop as refugee camps. They were small and in poor locations, very close to the border with Kosovo. The government-led reconnaissance was badly organized and chaotic, but I was able to meet with some key UN officials, in particular the head of the UNHCR mission to Kosovo, Jo Hegenauer, and the U.S. Ambassador at Large for War Crimes Issues, David Scheffer. I outlined my thoughts on the situation. In essence, someone was going to have to construct at least one major refugee camp. I advised that this should be near a grass airfield and range complex that we had discovered alongside the main road running from Pristina to Skopje, 10 kilometers south of the border crossing at Blace. The area was big enough to create humanitarian maneuver space to deal with the refugees, had a good river source for water, and was an excellent site for a logistics base. In the meantime, we agreed to help the Macedonian Government construct a small camp at Bojane, some 20 kilometers away.

Shortly afterwards, on 2nd April (Good Friday in the UK), I was contacted by Jo Hegenauer. Large numbers of Kosovar Albanians had been arriving at Blace over the last few days, by road and now by train, and things were getting extremely serious. There was no shelter, food, or medical cover, and the tired and hungry people were in a bad way; indeed, some were dying. They did not have the resources to do anything effective; could we help? I was in no doubt that we should do so. In my mind there were two imperatives. First, from my conversations with the Macedonian Government it was clear to me that they were in serious trouble, and a mass influx of refugees could be the catalyst for some form of collapse. This was the political military strategic issue. The Macedonian Government needed KFOR's strength, otherwise it would fall, and we needed them to maintain their resolve if we were not to find ourselves in the midst of a civil war. Alongside this strategic issue, however, was the humanitarian and moral imperative; there was a striking human catastrophe emerging.

There was no time to seek the views of others; the decision was mine alone. Over the previous 5 years, I had worked for the then KFOR Commander Lt. Gen. Mike Jackson on a number of deployments. I knew him well and had absolute confidence in him. While I was therefore pretty certain that he would back any decision I made, it has to be said that I was not so certain about the UK chain of command, and, somewhat unhelpfully, it was to them that I formally reported. My instinct was that if I attempted to get any timely clarity from the UK I would be sadly disappointed, and I might well have not liked any answers they did provide. While all commanders must understand their higher commanders intent if they are to make appropriate command decisions—and they should ideally have had the time to get to know each other well—I realized that I now needed to be prepared to make appropriate and timely decisions as these unexpected events unfolded, and then be prepared to live with the consequences.

I rang my Chief of Staff (COS) and ordered him to establish our tactical headquarters (Tac HQ) at the location near the airfield and implement the initial elements of our contingency plan. The immediate task was to establish a focal point where we could work with the UNHCR, ferrying food, blankets, and medical supplies up to the border. Tac HQ was up and running within 4 hours, and I ordered the release of both fresh food and operational rations. Our field kitchens started up and food was being moved forward by about 2300 hours on UNHCR vehicles loaded at our logistic base, some 9 hours after Jo Hegenauer's call. The temperature was not much above freezing, and it had been raining or sleeting for 36 hours. Images of the thousands of people crammed into the fields around the border crossing were beginning to be shown around the world. The scenes there were disturbingly chaotic, with no evidence of a coordinated response.

Pressure was mounting on the Macedonian Government, and on the UNHCR, whose small team was clearly going to be overwhelmed. Various government officials visited my Tac HQ during the following day, Saturday 3rd April—most importantly, in retrospect, Julia Taft from the U.S. State Department. The United States was putting real pressure on the Macedonian Government, who clearly needed convincing that the situation at Blace could not be allowed to continue. This was my next lesson: *forceful and effective diplomacy is essential at all stages of a complex emergency, and such diplomacy must be*

*sustained alongside any military options that are developed, even if
further discussions may at the time seem futile.*

While there was inevitably a great deal of uncertainty, as the hours
passed I became convinced that the dam at the border would break at
short notice, and when it did we had to be able to deal with the torrent
of refugees that would be released. The reality was that no other
organization was in a position to help. So, after a night of detailed
planning, I ordered major construction work to start.

The brigade engineers pulled aside the crop-spraying Antonov-2
aircraft, built a bridge across the fast-flowing stream that ran alongside
the airfield, opened up access tracks from our logistic base out onto the
range and airfield, and began to dig deep trench latrines. Elsewhere,
amongst a myriad of other tasks, the logistic regiment, working with
UNHCR, continued to move supplies forward to the border; the medics
began to prepare their reception centers, and the first tents were set up.
At 0800 hours on 4th April (Easter Sunday morning in the UK), the
Macedonian Deputy Foreign Minister , Boris Trajkovski, rang me to
ask that we should indeed implement our plan. International pressure,
particularly from the United States, had clearly worked. The tempo of
work increased. Water purifying and pumping systems were set up, and
reception and registration areas were established. General Jackson
visited and authorized assistance from other KFOR nations, and small
attachments from the German and Italian contingents arrived to help
put up tents. At 1700 hours, Macedonian police informed me that the
first refugees would be allowed across the border at 1900 hours. One of
the sites, eventually known as Stenkovic 1, was just about ready to
accept some, and overnight several hundred arrived. However, around
30,000 were estimated to be crammed into no-man's land at Blace, and
the situation there continued to deteriorate.

On Monday, 5th April, the dam broke. The UK Secretary of State for
International Development, Claire Short, arrived with the UK
Ambassador and a number of other officials; a large media presence
was also gathering. Authorizing DFID financial and political support,
which was to prove absolutely invaluable, she asked to look around. As
we were approaching the main airfield site, Stenkovic 2, a number of
buses arrived crammed to bursting point with refugees. The pictures of
Claire Short helping them off the buses became worldwide prime-time
news. Work continued but no more refugees arrived. Then darkness

fell. Suddenly buses by the dozen poured in. Arriving five at a time, with 80–100 refugees per bus, they disgorged their human loads and were replaced 15 minutes later by another 5 buses—and on it went, hour after hour. As dawn broke, the flow stopped, but by then around 20,000 refugees had arrived. All through the night soldiers from the brigade put up tents, helped families into them, issued food and blankets, and provided medical support. I watched as a tiny baby died, but many other refugees, both young and old, were successfully treated by the multinational medical facility. It was a grueling night, but it was just the first of many. Day after day, the brigade erected more tents and provided more water, food and other supplies. Night after night, the buses arrived. It was only later that we realized that during the day these buses were being used to ferry children in Skopje to and from school, and adults to and from work; as soon as it got dark they moved to the border to ply a different trade. By 9th April, there were around 40,000 refugees in the two major camps; while some were being flown out there was little space left.

Over 2,800 tents had been erected, 1,600 meters of water pipeline had been laid, and tens of thousands of meals had been cooked and distributed, along with over 103,000 jars of baby food, 11,000 loaves of bread, 264,000 liters of bottled water and 430,000 bars of chocolate; 400 deep-trench latrines had been dug and thousands of refugees had been treated in our medical facilities—five died, but 24 babies were born, our proudest statistic!

In one sense the worst was over. Initially, the NGO presence on the ground had been minimal. OXFAM arrived first, and quickly became effective, playing a key role in the development of the water and sanitation systems. Other organizations began to arrive, but slowly. The UN became more effective as the weeks progressed. Various senior officials arrived and were briefed, the UNHCR and WFP teams were strengthened, and several key individuals emerged as real "players." For a few days the flow of refugees slowed, and the various NGOs finally began to get organized, which helped to release some of the pressure on my military assets. Coordinating their activities was far from easy, but on Sunday 11th April, we were able to hand over most of the medical support to MSF and the Red Cross. Although we began to plan the hand-over of all aspects of the camps, the following week was still a demanding one. The camps had to be extended as more refugees arrived, policing and security became a problem, and the temperatures began to soar. Rubbish clearance, sanitation, and the threat of disease became key issues; once again our military resources had to lead the way. Further influxes of refugees continued, and thunder storms flooded the camps. The ability of the various agencies to cope remained suspect, and we were asked, by the UNHCR, to stay on for a few more days. Finally, we withdrew over the period of the 17th–19th April, leaving behind a military liaison team.

After a gap of about 8 days, during which time the brigade was immersed in the RSOI of the 2nd Battlegroup and the training program of 4 Armoured Brigade, our attention was directed back to the humanitarian aspects of the situation once again. Inside Kosovo, additional waves of Kosovar Albanians were being rounded up and moved to the borders. The camps in Macedonia were full, and the ones in Northern Albania, where NATO AFOR was operating, were overflowing. The Macedonian Government was adamant that it would not allow additional camps to be built in their central and southern regions, and so attention focused on southern Albania. Numerous meetings were held and reconnaissance trips conducted. Finally, UNHCR and HQ KFOR agreed that we should use brigade assets to establish a series of camps in the Korce region of Albania, around 40 kilometers south of Lake Ochrid. Dividing the brigade, and the HQ, over such a distance—we would now have elements of the brigade in three countries, Greece, Macedonia and Albania—was far from ideal. My main HQ was heavily involved with military support to KFOR, particularly 4 Armoured Brigade, and our primary mission was to support the UK move into Kosovo. Nonetheless, there seemed little likelihood of any such move in the short term. Indeed, we were beginning to plan forced entry options, which would inevitably take weeks to prepare and implement. The lead elements of Tac HQ thus deployed to Albania on 8th May, and I joined my COS there the next day.

The problems were very different to those we had encountered in Macedonia over Easter. Although there was a time imperative, it was not as urgent as before. The UNHCR and NGO presence was considerable, and the emphasis was on developing sustainable camps suitable for refugees to live in throughout the winter, if necessary. It was, however, a demanding few weeks. Local politics was riven with corruption, and there was criminality in abundance. Superimposed on this was an unclear military command structure—we were operating in

AFOR's area of responsibility, with both AFOR and KFOR forces working with us—and an equally unclear link between the UNHCR in Albania and Macedonia. Our first few situation reports apparently read more like a John Le Carré novel than a military update, particularly when rival gangs in Korce began open warfare, and anticorruption officials, appointed from Tirana, began to stir things up. Nonetheless, by 6th June, and in very close concert with DFID, the UNHCR, and the NGOs, four substantial camps were constructed, and other locations surveyed and planned. In all, we created capacity for well over 60,000 refugees. As it turned out only 12,000–15,000 spaces were used as, once again, events were to turn. This time they turned for the better.

At the beginning of June, planning for the B option had begun in earnest, and additional elements of the brigade, still based in UK, were deployed. At short notice, 5 Airborne Brigade and a large RAF Support Helicopter force were in-loaded and configured to go north into Kosovo. Entry into Force was 10th June, D-Day 12th June. By 18th June, my Tac HQ had moved up into Pristina, along with literally hundreds of journalists and NGOs, of every acronym imaginable. In addition to providing military engineering, logistic, and medical support to the UK Forces, the brigade repaired and ran a large part of the Kosovo railway system, and established a firefighting capability in Pristina and a civilian criminal detention centre in Lipljan. In addition, a temporary, emergency refugee camp was constructed just outside Pristina to enable several thousand Romany gypsies to be relocated. In all of these areas we attempted, with lesser or greater success, to work with the various non-military organizations and agencies, which by then were pouring into Kosovo. Individual relationships were excellent, but tensions between KFOR and the UNHCR at the operational level meant that the brigade's assets were under-utilized, particularly our rail capability. By the beginning of August, the situation was settling, and we began to prepare to hand over our responsibilities. We finally withdrew and returned to the UK in late August.

This deployment was, without doubt, a turning point in my understanding of the changing nature of conflict. In some respects there is nothing new in any operation, but I came away convinced that the pendulum had swung firmly away from using just military force to bring a conflict decisively to an end. The end of the Cold War had seen an alarming increase in the number of complex emergencies around the world, and these conflicts had resulted in historically high levels of military commitment. Military commanders were clearly having to work ever more closely with non-military organizations and agencies. The deployment to Macedonia/Albania/Kosovo was but one example of this trend, with 101 Logistic Brigade leading the NATO/KFOR response to the developing humanitarian crisis.

It became clear to me that there are significant differences between the military and humanitarian agencies, both in structure and approach. These reflect our respective missions, expectations, values, and perceptions, but above all our psyche and professional ethos. While these differences are significant, and will certainly not disappear, on balance I came to the conclusion that the tensions can be creative, not disruptive. This is not, or at least should not be, a battle between "bloody hands" and "bleeding hearts." Both sides have weaknesses, but both bring real strengths to bear. The trick is to understand and accept the differences, bring together the positive strengths, and focus them on overcoming the crisis, be it man-made or natural.

It is important to recognize that the military role is to support, not supplant, the work of the non-military players; we are there to serve, not to be served. The establishment of a secure environment, along with logistic, medical and engineering support—encompassing the management of airheads and seaports, transportation, shelter and route protection—are all key roles. Our collective and joint doctrine must reflect agreed principles on everything from intelligence gathering and analysis, provision of the means, including funding, the roles of the military, and the links with and status of non-military aid agencies and civilian contractors. Ideally, there is a need for an integrated campaign plan, covering the political, economic, legal, and humanitarian imperatives, alongside the military ones. While inevitably events on the ground will dictate and modify, and commanders will need to respond to these changes, such a campaign plan, prepared jointly by the key players using a framework set within an agreed doctrine, will guide and educate, support, and, where necessary, constrain.

There is certainly much work to be done, particularly in the areas of education, training, and doctrine, if we are to better orchestrate and execute more effective joint action. This will not be easy, but the realities of these deployments is that the various players, including government departments, must enhance their links and work more closely with each other, and with the other key players, agencies, and donors. Through understanding and patient leadership, strong relationships can and should be developed. The two halves of the humanitarian operation have the potential to form a strong and effective team.

Essay 9

Retaining the Lessons of Nation-Building

By James Dobbins

Observing America's first year in Iraq, one might be forgiven for thinking that this was the first time that the United States had embarked upon such an enterprise. In fact, this was the seventh occasion in little more than a decade that the United States had helped liberate a society and then tried to rebuild it, beginning with Kuwait in 1991, and then Somalia, Haiti, Bosnia, Kosovo, Afghanistan, and finally Iraq. Six of these seven societies are dominantly Muslim.

Thus, by 2003, there was no army in the world more experienced in nation-building than the American, and no Western army with more modern experience operating within a Muslim society. How, one might ask, could the United States perform this mission so frequently, yet do it so poorly? The answer is that neither the American military nor any of the relevant civilian agencies had regarded post-conflict stabilization and reconstruction as a core function, to be adequately funded, regularly practiced, and routinely executed. Instead, the U.S. Government had tended to treat each of these missions as if it were the first ever encountered, sending new people with new ideas to face what should have been familiar challenges. Worse yet, it treated each mission as if it were the last such it would ever have to do. No agency was taking steps to harvest and sustain the expertise gained. No one was establishing an evolving doctrine for the conduct of these operations, or building a cadre of experts available to go from one mission to the next.

Since the end of the Korean War, America's conventional battles have ended in a matter of days in overwhelming victories with few if any friendly casualties. Nation-building, counterinsurgency, and post-conflict reconstruction, on the other hand, have always proved much more time-consuming, expensive, and problematic. One reason for this disjunction is that the U.S. Government is well structured for peace or war, but ill-adapted for missions that fall somewhere in between. In both peace and conventional war, each agency knows its place. Coordination between agencies, while demanding, does not call for endless improvisation. By contrast, nation-building, stability operations, counterinsurgency, and irregular warfare all require that agencies collaborate in ways to which they are not accustomed. Consequently, these missions are among the most difficult for any President to direct. The U.S. Government simply is not structured for the purpose.

Administrations get better at these types of operations as they gain experience. Unfortunately, their improved capacity does not automatically carry over to their successors. The expertise acquired has been developed on an ad hoc and largely personal basis, and is not built into the relevant institutions. Therefore, it can be easily lost. One can trace this process of progress and regression in the decade following the end of the Cold War, which saw an upsurge in nation-building-type missions.

Nation-Building

During his 8 years in office President Clinton oversaw four successive efforts at stabilization and post-conflict reconstruction. Beginning with an unqualified failure in Somalia, followed by a largely wasted effort in Haiti, his administration was eventually able to achieve more enduring results in Bosnia and Kosovo. Each successive operation was better conceived and more competently conducted than its predecessor, as the same officials repeatedly preformed comparable tasks.

The Clinton administration derived three large policy lessons from its experience: employ overwhelming force, prepare to accept responsibility for the provision of public security, and engage neighboring and regional states, particularly those making the most trouble.

Overwhelming force should be applied until security is established

In Somalia, President George H.W. Bush originally had sent a large American force to do a very limited task: protecting humanitarian food and medicine shipments. Bill Clinton reduced that American presence from 20,000 soldiers and marines to 2,000, and gave the residual force the mission of supporting a UN–led, grass roots democratization campaign that was bound to antagonize every warlord in the country. This sent capabilities plummeting even as ambitions soared. The reduced American force was soon challenged. The encounter chronicled in the book and movie "Blackhawk Down" resulted in a firestorm of domestic criticism and caused the administration to withdraw American troops from Somalia.

From then on, the Clinton administration embraced the "Powell doctrine" of applying overwhelming force, choosing to super-size each of its subsequent interventions, going in heavy and then scaling back once potential adversaries had been deterred from mounting violent resistance and a secure environment had been established.

Planners and policymakers should assume the responsibility for public security until local forces can meet the local security challenge

In Somalia, Haiti, and Kosovo, the United States had arrived to find local security forces incompetent, abusive, or nonexistent. Building new institutions and reforming existing ones took several years (and in Somalia was not even seriously attempted). In the interim, responsibility for public security devolved on the United States and its coalition partners. The U.S. military resisted this mission, to no avail. By 1999, when they went into Kosovo, U.S. and NATO military authorities accepted that the responsibility for public safety would be a military task until international and local police could be mobilized in sufficient numbers.

Engage all neighboring parties, including those that are most obstructive

Neighboring states played a major role in fomenting the conflicts in Somalia, Bosnia, and Kosovo. This problem was largely ignored in Somalia, but faced squarely in Bosnia. The Presidents of Serbia and

Croatia, both of whom bore heavy responsibility for the ethnic cleansing that NATO was trying to stop, were invited by the United States to the peace conference in Dayton, Ohio. Both men were given privileged places in that process, and continued to be engaged in the subsequent peace implementation. Both men won subsequent elections in their own countries, their domestic stature having been enhanced by their exalted international roles. Had Washington treated them as pariahs, the war in Bosnia might be underway still.

By 1999, the Serbian leader, Slobodan Milosevic, had actually been indicted by the international tribunal in The Hague for genocide and other war crimes. Yet, NATO and the Clinton administration negotiated with his regime again to end the air campaign and the conflict in Kosovo.

Starting Over

Each of these lessons was rejected by a successor U.S. administration initially determined to avoid nation-building altogether, and subsequently insistent on doing it entirely differently, and in particular more economically.

Ironically, the Powell doctrine of overwhelming force had been embraced only after General Powell left office in 1993, and was abandoned as soon as he returned in 2001. Secretary of Defense Rumsfeld's views were diametrically opposed. He argued in speeches and op-ed articles that flooding Bosnia and Kosovo with military manpower and economic assistance had turned these societies into permanent wards of the international community. The Bush administration, he explained, by stinting on such commitments, would ensure that Afghanistan and Iraq more quickly become self-sufficient. This line of thinking transposed the American domestic debate over welfare reform to the international arena. The analogy could not have proven less apt. By making minimal initial efforts at stabilization in Afghanistan and Iraq, and then reinforcing its commitments of manpower and money only once challenged, the Bush administration failed to deter the emergence of organized resistance in either country. The Rumsfeld vision of defense transformation proved well suited to conventional combat against vastly inferior adversaries, but turned out to be a much more expensive approach to post-conflict stabilization and reconstruction.

During the 2000 Presidential campaign, Condoleezza Rice wrote dismissively of stability operations, declaring that "we don't need to have the 82nd Airborne escorting kids to kindergarten." Consistent with this view, the Bush administration, having overthrown the Taliban and installed a new government in Kabul, determined that American troops would do no peacekeeping in that country, and that peacekeepers from other countries would not be allowed to venture beyond the Kabul city limits. Public security throughout the rest of the country was to be left entirely to the Afghans, despite the fact that Afghanistan had no army and no police force. A year later, President Bush was asking his advisers irritably why such reconstruction as had occurred was largely limited to the capital.

The same attitude toward public security informed U.S. plans for post-invasion Iraq. Washington assumed that Iraqi police and military would continue to maintain public order after Saddam's regime was removed. The fact that this had proved impossible not just in Afghanistan a year earlier, but also in Somalia, Haiti, and Kosovo, was ignored. In the weeks leading up to the invasion, the Pentagon leadership cut the number of military police proposed for the operation by U.S. military authorities, while the White House cut even more drastically the number of international civilian police proposed by the State Department. Lest there be any doubt that these police were not to do policing, the White House also directed that any civilian police sent to Iraq should be unarmed. For the next several years, as Iraq descended into civil war, American authorities declined to collect data on the number of Iraqis getting killed. Secretary Rumsfeld maintained that such statistics were not a relevant indicator of the success or failure of the American military mission. Only with the arrival of General Petraeus in 2007 did the number of civilian casualties become the chief metric for measuring the progress of the campaign.

America's quick success in overthrowing the Taliban and replacing it with a broadly based government owed much to the assistance received from nearby states, including such long-term opponents of the Taliban as Iran, Russia, and India. Yet, no sooner had the Karzai government been installed than Washington rebuffed offers of further assistance from Iran and relaxed the pressure on Pakistan to sever its remaining ties with violent extremists groups. The broad regional strategy, so critical to both Washington's initial military victory and political achievement, was effectively abandoned.

A regional strategy was not even attempted with respect to Iraq. The invasion was conducted not just against the advice of several of Washington's most important allies, but also contrary to the wishes of most regional states. With the exception of Kuwait, none of Iraq's neighbors supported the intervention. Even Kuwait cannot have been enthusiastic about the announced American intention to make Iraq a democratic model for the region in the hopes of inspiring similar changes in the form of government of all its neighbors. Not surprisingly, neighborly interference quickly became a significant factor in stoking Iraq's sectarian passions.

In his second term, President Bush worked hard to recover from these early mistakes. In the process, his administration embraced the mission of post-conflict stabilization with the fervor of a new convert. The President issued a new directive setting out an interagency structure for managing such operations. Secretary of State Rice recanted her earlier dismissal of nation-building. The State Department established an Office of Reconstruction and Stabilization charged with establishing a doctrine for the civilian conduct of such missions and building a cadre of experts ready to man them. The Defense Department issued a directive making stability operations a core function of the American military.

In Iraq, more forces and money were committed, public security was embraced as the heart of a new counterinsurgency strategy, and efforts were made to better engage neighboring states, not even excepting Iran. The lessons of the 1990s had been relearned, and Iraq was pulled back from the abyss.

Retaining Hard Won Lessons

The 2008 American elections returned a new President of a different party, and consequently offered every prospect of another abrupt fall off this hard-won learning curve. Fortunately, President Obama decided to keep Robert Gates as Secretary of Defense, General David Petraeus at Central Command, and Lieutenant General Douglas Lute, along with a team of professional military, diplomatic, and intelligence officers advising him and organizing the interagency management of both wars. The result has been a degree of continuity that leaves some Democrats uneasy, but offers hope that the lessons of the past two decades will not be lost once again in the transition from one administration and governing party to the next.

As articulated so far, the Obama strategy for Afghanistan is an effort to replicate the success achieved in Iraq in 2007 by employing many of the same elements: a counterinsurgency doctrine focused on public security, increases in U.S. and Afghan military manpower needed to execute such a mission, financial incentives to economically motivated insurgents to change sides, intensified regional diplomacy—particularly with Pakistan, but also Iran, Russia and India—and a willingness to envisage accommodation with some elements of the insurgency. President Obama has sought to distinguish his approach rhetorically from that of his predecessor by downplaying nation-building and focusing instead on counterterrorism as the reason for being in Afghanistan. Yet he accompanied this apparent narrowing of the American mission by increasing manpower and money devoted to it. Further, the President's immediate rational for an increase in American troop strength was the need to secure the upcoming Afghan elections. Nation-building thus remains at the core of the American strategy for Afghanistan (and Iraq), even if the term is still officially eschewed.

While the Bush administration made a start, after 2005, in building institutional capacity for stability operations, much still needs to be done if the current level of expertise is not to degrade again after the immediate crises recede. Forestalling such a regression will require the establishment, by legislation, of an enduring division of labor between the White House, State, Defense, and USAID. There must be an allocation of responsibilities that cannot be lightly altered by each passing administration, for no agency will invest in activities it may not long need to carry out.

In assigning these responsibilities, the role of the White House should be to set policy and make sure agencies adhere to it. The role of the State Department should be to ensure that all programs conducted overseas, by any agency, support the President's policies and are optimized to achieve his objectives. The Defense Department should execute only those programs for which the military has a comparative advantage. Other programs should be executed by civilian agencies— the default agency should be a reformed and expanded USAID, which should be given cabinet status and renamed the Department for Development and Reconstruction. But control over funding for all non-military activities conducted in stabilization missions should remain with State, as this is the only means that agency has to play its assigned role as the operational link between a policy-setting White House and the multiple program-executing agencies.

America's experience in Afghanistan and Iraq has illustrated the costs of unprepared nation-building. The cost of sustaining the capacity to conduct these operations, and thus retaining the lessons of the past two decades, is trivial by comparison.

Essay 10

Missions Accomplished and Unaccomplished

By Jan Eliasson

My background in complex international operations is mainly in the area of mediation and peacekeeping under the auspices of the United Nations or a regional organization.

I have been the Personal Representative of the UN Secretary General during the Iran/Iraq conflict, the Special Envoy of the UN in the Darfur conflict, and the chief mediator in the Nagorno-Karabakh conflict for the OSCE (Organization for Security and Co-operation in Europe). I also have conducted humanitarian diplomacy in crisis situations in the Horn of Africa (Sudan and Somalia) and in Myanmar/Burma, dealing with issues such as opening humanitarian corridors and repatriation of refugees.

This is an attempt to draw some general conclusions and formulate some lessons learned from these experiences, spanning a period of over 25 years. I shall also attempt to identify some specific trends in conflict resolution and in the organization of operations in crisis areas.

Cooperation With Parties and Among Actors

No conflict can be terminated without a minimum of cooperation and political will among the parties. There are examples of imposed solutions, but such solutions tend to be short-lived, fragile, and fraught with built-in tensions.

In my view, too few efforts are required to learn about and deal with political, economic, social, and cultural roots and causes of conflicts. Some interventions demonstrate lack of cultural sensitivity, and even blatant lack of respect for the history and traditions of foreign countries. Much more attention must be given to enhancing cultural understanding and adequately preparing and training personnel heading for complex operations.

It is also important to constantly be aware of the need to maintain balanced and fair contacts with all parties to the conflict. The party representing a government in civil war situations is usually well organized and easily available to mediators. It is, however, equally essential to be in close contact with opposition movements, which often are dispersed or splintered and lack the resources of a government apparatus.

To deal effectively with the parties in complex crises, it is increasingly necessary to cooperate with other relevant organizations and actors. In the Darfur crisis it has proved indispensable to have close cooperation between the UN and the regional organization, in this case, the African Union (AU). This cooperation includes both mediation and peacekeeping operations. For 18 months, I worked closely with Dr. Salim Ahmed Salim of the AU. In July 2007, Resolution 1769 of the UN Security Council confirmed a merger between the AU and UN peacekeeping operations.

The role of regional arrangements was foreseen in the UN Charter in 1946. Chapter VIII underlines the responsibility of regional actors to find solutions to conflicts, even before they reach the UN Security Council. There is clearly a great, underutilized potential for cooperation between international and regional organizations. Such cooperation, however, is not without problems. There are differing cultures and traditions as well as varying circumstances when it comes to training and financing of operations. A major issue that cries out for solutions is whether regional peacekeeping operations can be financed by assessed contributions from the UN. In my view, this should be possible when a regional organization is acting on a mandate assigned by the UN Security Council. This should be a concrete and meaningful way to reflect the spirit and letter of chapter VIII of the UN Charter.

A Comprehensive Approach to Peacemaking, Peacekeeping, and Peacebuilding

To effectively carry out complex operations, a comprehensive approach is necessary. By this I mean that peacemaking, peacekeeping, and peacebuilding should be combined and seen as one process. This assures a long-term perspective on the operation and requires close coordination of political, military, economic, and social efforts to stabilize situations and make real nation-building possible. There is no peace without development, there is no development without peace, and there is no lasting peace and development without respect for human rights.

This, of course, also requires institution-building and a measure of good governance in the conflict area or affected country. There has to be a combination of effective action from the outside and sufficient absorption capacity and political will in the country concerned (see the results in Afghanistan today).

When it comes to Darfur, I would go as far as to say that peace will continue to be elusive as long as the interplay and coordination between peacemaking, peacekeeping, and peacebuilding is deficient or absent. A serious mediation effort requires not only effective peacekeeping to stabilize the situation, but also concrete plans for peacebuilding in the form of recovery and reconstruction programs. In addition, there should also be credible efforts by the central government to achieve social and economic development for all parts and citizens of the country after a political settlement.

To illustrate, around a billion dollars is spent in Darfur every year on humanitarian assistance to a population of 2.4 million internally displaced persons (IDPs) and another 1.5 million people in impoverished areas in Darfur. This enormous operation, involving over 12,000 humanitarian workers, is almost exclusively aimed at the daily survival of this population by supplying food, medicine, water, and basic necessities.

Very little, if any, of this assistance goes to recovery and reconstruction programs preparing for future peace in Darfur. Admittedly, such programs are difficult to implement while conflict continues, as is the case in several parts of Darfur. But there are areas where relative stability prevails and conditions for normalization could be created. Progress toward stability could be achieved by drilling wells for water in the distant and dried-out villages, setting up modest health clinics, and opening a country school and building a road between two towns, thereby giving jobs to demobilized soldiers and militia.

Not only would such programs—which would yield results within 6–12 months—provide a degree of dignity to hundreds of thousands of people, they would also create incentives for and pressures on the parties to the conflict to sit down at the negotiation table and find formulas for a peaceful settlement. They would not have to prove to or convince their followers that peace pays off, or that it is a better proposition than continued war.

The comprehensive approach also includes the growing need to involve and take into account civil society in peacemaking and peacebuilding. Civil society's involvement in peace processes is indispensable and reflects the need for public support during and after a peace process. Civil society is often a lobby for peaceful solutions and plays an important role—together with the media—in molding public opinion with regard to the international presence in complex operations. However there are situations where NGOs are seen as being partial or leaning in favor of one of the parties. If an international organization or a mediator tends to rely on such NGOs—even if they have justified causes and motives—their own neutrality and credibility may be endangered.

Reflections on Darfur and Mediation

Dr. Salim and I started our cooperation as mediators for the AU and UN in the Darfur conflict in December 2006. We made substantial progress in the middle of 2007 mainly due to two developments:

- UN Security Council Resolution 1769 of July 31, 2007, which established a strong link between the UN and the AU, particularly in peacekeeping; and

- the common platform for negotiations elaborated by seven of the eight most important movements in Darfur, which was met by the Government of Sudan with serious interest.

However, the situation in Darfur, Sudan, and the region deteriorated drastically during the following few months. In early September 2007, one of the most important movements, the Justice and Equality Movement (JEM), split into two competing factions. One splinter group chose to cooperate with the UN and AU, while the other, led by JEM founder Khalil Ibrahim, declined the invitation to start the talks in Sirte, Libya, in October 2007, and rejected the inclusive invitation to all movement factions.

In October 2007, the SPLM (Sudan Peoples' Liberation Movement) of the Government of National Unity (GNU) in Khartoum chose to suspend the work in government with the leading National Congress Party (NCP). The tensions between the coalition partners had grown considerably during the preceding few months. This development further complicated the dialogue with the Government of Sudan on the Darfur issue.

Relations between Chad and Sudan took a negative turn at the end of 2007, commencing with several border clashes, which were followed by mutual accusations of meddling in each other's internal affairs. The important Zagawa tribe is as strong in Chad as it is in Darfur, and tribal loyalties extend across the border. In fact, peace in Darfur can hardly be achieved without normalization between Chad and Sudan. This became tragically evident in the spring of 2008 when the capital of Chad, N'Djamena was attacked and, later, when Undurman, a suburb of Khartoum, was surrounded by groups loyal or close to the government in Chad.

These events led me to the following conclusions when I reported to the UN Security Council in New York on June 24, 2008. Peace in Darfur cannot be achieved, if:

- there is not a minimum of unity in the Security Council, and if the Council's resolutions are not implemented (Resolution 1769 was seriously lacking in this regard at that time);

- the neighbors of Sudan—notably Chad, Libya, Eritrea, and Egypt—are not pulling in the same direction (which was not the case);

- the Government of Sudan is not truly working as a Government of National Unity (the GNU was far from a reality);

- the movements are splintered and cannot unify, or at least choose a common negotiation team for the peace talks (they had tried and failed, and been boycotted by a major, Paris-based movement, the Sudan Liberation Movement, led by Abdul Wahid el-Nur).

These reflections underline the fact that a mediator has limited possibilities to reach a peaceful solution without the active support of major powers and neighboring countries, and without the parties' genuine interest in a political settlement. During my mediation efforts in different parts of the world, I often thought of myself as a man trying to bring horses to a waterhole, and then finding that they do not want to drink. Has anyone ever successfully forced a horse to drink?

Peace efforts must be pursued simultaneously on several levels, and in several dimensions, if positive and lasting results are to be achieved in today's world of complex crises and operations.

The Politics of Complex Operations

By James Kunder

While serving as Director of the Office of U.S. Foreign Disaster Assistance at USAID, I was ordered to Somalia in November 1992, when that nation was in the throes of a major humanitarian and political crisis. In January, 2002, while working as a private consultant, I was asked to rejoin the U.S. Government and was ordered to Afghanistan to reopen the USAID mission there. Aside from these two deployments, from the early 1990s until leaving USAID in January 2009, I conducted assessment missions or managed government or non-governmental programs in a range of complex operations venues, including Angola, Bosnia, Colombia, Georgia, Iraq, Liberia, Mozambique, Nicaragua, Sri Lanka, Sudan, and the West Bank/Gaza. From these varied experiences I have distilled three lessons I would like to share in this essay.

Let me begin in a spirit of sincere humility. Complex operations are, as the term suggests, inherently difficult. My Chief of Mission when I arrived in Kabul, Ryan Crocker, had previously served as U.S. ambassador to Pakistan, Syria, and Lebanon, before going on to high achievement in Iraq. Ambassador Crocker was fond of noting the number of difficult assignments he and I had attempted before arriving in Kabul, then dryly joking that, "it is obvious Jim and I will continue to be sent to these places until we get it right!" That is to say, I recognize that whatever lessons learned I convey here can serve only as data points, not formulas, for those grappling with complex operations in the future.

My first observation or lesson is that every one of these complex operations in which I have served was, pure and simple, a political event. Now, it may seem unnecessary to state this simple lesson, but I do so for a purpose: to urge that we practitioners in complex operations not become excessively enamored of technique, or prisoners of our own elegant programs. Let me elaborate.

One of the positive developments in complex operations in recent decades is progress in the techniques available to practitioners, both civilian and military. To our credit, we have developed military doctrine to enshrine the advantages of working closely with civilian partners. Commanders now arrive at the site of complex operations with Commander's Emergency Response Program (CERP) funds to address local community needs. USAID has developed stand-by rosters of specialists in complex operations, a precursor to a much expanded Civilian Response Corps, We link State, Defense, and USAID personnel in provincial reconstruction teams. And the linkages between demobilized fighters, jobs, and recruitment are better delineated. This list of enhanced techniques could be extended. In short, the civilian crisis manager or military commander shows up at a complex operation today with a much more effective toolkit than his or her predecessor of just two decades ago.

The downside of having this 21st-century toolkit is that we spend a very large amount of time, from the highest levels of the U.S. Government to the most isolated forward operating base, sorting through our tools for the array of programs that we will employ. And each tool in the kit has a bureaucratic constituency. Will we focus on microenterprise job creation to offset the recruitment appeal of insurgent groups? What increment of additional power generation will best promote restoration of stability? Are the critical ministries functioning properly, with good financial accounting systems and home-grown inspectors general? Are we tracking revenue collection closely enough? Now, all of these issues, in a given complex operation, may be important, even essential. But they may also cloud the essentially political nature of the crisis.

In each of the complex operations in which I have served, I have been struck by the deep-rootedness of the underlying political conflict that spawned the complex crisis. The political conflict often goes to the heart of identity issues, those dynamics—driven by religion, ethnicity, tribe, clan, language, heritage—that are close to the core of the human condition. And, although complex operations practitioners can apply their program and budget toolbox to ameliorating such issues, neither programmatic interventions nor better program coordination can substitute for addressing underlying political conflict. Let me give a concrete example.

While deployed to Bosnia in 1991–92, I had occasion to observe residents destroying Yugos, the compact automobile that had been the pride of the former Federal Republic of Yugoslavia. Now, Yugos may not have run that well, but they were produced in factories where laborers received wages comparable to those paid in Western Europe, and the destruction of the market for the cars—as well as the cars themselves—made absolutely no rational sense by the standards of complex operations practitioners. We wanted to create high-paying jobs, in the familiar logic, so that people would have hope for the future and put aside their inter-ethnic difficulties. But here was a society that was destroying high-paying jobs by destroying Yugos—hence suppressing the market for them—because the name of the automobile conjured up a political entity with which they no longer identified.

In a world where political issues, and underlying issues of human identity, produce such counterintuitive results, it is essential that complex operations address the political issues head-on to achieve stability. A positive trend in both Afghanistan and Iraq, in my view, is the new policy of incorporating three to five individuals carrying full ambassadorial rank into the senior leadership of the U.S. embassies. We need more senior diplomats, buttressed by strong language skills, on the site of complex operations. But this is only a down payment. Developing a sound, complex operations strategy for Afghanistan, for example, requires a substantial national investment in understanding Pashtun nationalism and the reaction that nationalism provokes in Hazaras, Uzbeks, Tajiks, and others. There is no shortcut, no elegant combination of employment programs and donor coordination centers, that will stabilize the country without taking on the underlying political conflicts of Afghanistan. In this sense, Afghanistan is like every other complex operation.

The second lesson I would like to share from my experience in complex operations is the imperative that we get serious about effective civilian command and control in reconstruction and stabilization operations. In my view, the current state of coordination among civilian agencies–American, other governments, international agencies, the UN, the NGOs and private contractors, the Red Cross/Red Crescent movement, and, not least, the government we are supposedly trying to help–veers between tragedy and farce, and always exhibits chaos. The costs of under-coordinated civilian response, in delay, wasted motion, and funds are apparent in many complex operations. This is an area ripe for improvement.

Let me be clear about what I mean by effective civilian command and control in complex operations. I am not addressing the issue of conflict between civilian and military policy, nor suggesting that civilian agencies need more control over military forces in complex operations. The necessity of integrating civilian and military policy is a serious issue that deserves further attention, but that is not the point here. Rather, the command and control issue that, in my observation, most needs attention is ensuring that the many civilian reconstruction and stabilization agencies that operate in a complex operation synchronize their efforts. Minimal coordination among civilian agencies is the rule in most complex operations, and the costs of minimal coordination are high. Moreover, the highest-profile complex crises with the highest strategic stakes often draw the largest number of outside civilian organizations, thus exacerbating coordination issues precisely where synergy is most needed.

Let me return to Afghanistan for an example. The numerous civilian agencies operating there cannot perfectly harmonize their reconstruction and stabilization efforts, but they can, at the absolute minimum, maintain a standard, transparent database indicating where and on what they are working in order to avoid duplication. The need for a centralized civilian agency database of projects and programs was recognized in Afghanistan soon after Coalition forces arrived in 2001. In 2002, donors, led by the U.S. government, created a reconstruction data center in the Afghan Finance Ministry to serve as a central clearinghouse of civilian projects. But, as recently as May 2009, a senior United Nations official in Kabul reported to me that several major donors do not even report their program data to the Finance Ministry, which renders the data hub only minimally useful as a coordination tool.

This example barely scratches the surface of the problem. There is, in reality, no accepted system of civilian agency coordination during complex operations. The closest that practitioners come in most complex operations is a degree of voluntary coalescing around the leadership of the United Nations, especially when the severity of the crisis leads to the appointment of a Special Representative of the Secretary-General (SRSG). Even this arrangement tends to fray when the international response to a complex operation is a "coalition of the willing," as opposed to a formal UN peacekeeping mission under chapters VI or VII of the UN Charter.

The problem of civilian coordination is profound. Simply put, there is no global legal, doctrinal, treaty, or other basis on which to establish an authoritative command and control wiring diagram when a complex operation begins. There is no civilian NATO. The large, bilateral donor nations (the United States included) that arrive at a crisis venue with deep pockets and their own technical reconstruction staff often determine their reconstruction priorities based on direction from their capitals. The International Committee of the Red Cross, or other elements of the Red Cross/Red Crescent movement, may have a large presence, but they report neither to the UN nor to any bilateral donor. The UN agencies sometimes barely coordinate between themselves. The major multilateral financial institutions, like the World Bank, often strive to establish–with the best of intentions–their own coordination centers and processes. Non-governmental organizations and civilian contractors may cluster around combinations of each category of donors as funding support becomes available for one priority or another. Often at the periphery of all this activity is the entity that should be at the center of the action: the government of the country in crisis. As is widely recognized, outside troops and civilian agencies are likely to leave a complex operation only once the host-nation government is functioning.

Efforts have been undertaken to solve this civilian coordination conundrum. In the complex operations I have observed, various combinations have been tried with varying degrees of success. These include strenuous efforts by the SRSG to establish central control, creation of a range of "trust funds" coordinated by a central team into which donor agencies can make contributions, creation of donor coordination centers or humanitarian operations centers, and establishment of sectoral councils (for employment, health, education, transportation, energy, and other sectors), with each council headed by the relevant minister of the host-nation government. But none of these mechanisms has achieved more than limited or passing success.

Ineffective command and control of civilian agencies is an unfortunate but ubiquitous feature of complex operations.

My third lesson is that practitioners–and I include myself–often pay too little attention to success stories and invest too little time in disseminating information on what works. In workshops and after-action reviews I have noticed a disproportionate focus on a limited number of case studies—Afghanistan, Iraq, Bosnia, and Rwanda come to mind. It is perhaps natural to focus on the most interesting or compelling case studies, especially those in which U.S. or other foreign troops played a major role. Unfortunately, interesting and compelling cases often are those in which something did not work very well. In my view, there are a number of quite successful strategic and tactical responses to complex crises in places like El Salvador, the Philippines (especially Mindanao), Mozambique, and even Tajikistan. I have seldom encountered serious discussions of these examples.

In Mozambique, the brutality and tribal nature of the long civil war during the 1980s and 1990s made prospects for a successful resolution seem bleak. Now Mozambique is a relatively successful model of stability and economic growth in southern Africa. The intercommunal, peacebuilding techniques employed there, and the role played by an international religious organization with contacts on both sides of the fighting (the Community of Sant Egidio), are elements that could be usefully studied by complex operations practitioners.

El Salvador, in my view, is an extraordinarily useful model of how a carefully negotiated peace agreement that addresses underlying issues of exclusion and political repression can serve as a catalyst for peace and stability. El Salvador is not without problems, but, the decades of violence there from the 1930s to the 1980s, and the historical dynamic of ethnicity and Marxism, made peace seem a distant prospect during many of those years. The peace treaty ending the civil war is an extraordinary and voluminous document that addresses issues ranging from reconstitution of the security forces, to land reform and political access, to the establishment of truth commissions for those accused of atrocities during the fighting.

In my experience, I seldom hear discussion of these positive case studies as examples that might usefully impact an Iraq or an Afghanistan, even though I have heard some thoughtful analysts suggest that Mindanao is perhaps the single best example worldwide of successful coordination between military counterinsurgency operations and development/reconstruction efforts. As lessons learned in the field of complex operations are developed further, it would be worthwhile to examine carefully such lesser-known examples of successful attempts to address problems of failed states, complex contingencies, and integrated civilian-military interventions.

Reconstructing Post-Conflict Reconstruction: Lessons from Iraq

By Lewis W. Lucke

I began my association with USAID's Iraq planning effort in late October 2002. I had previously been USAID Mission Director in three countries including Jordan (1996–2000), and thus was one of the few senior USAID officials with extensive Middle East experience. I had also studied Arabic for several years in the United States and Jordan. I retired from USAID just prior to September 11, 2001, but rejoined USAID post-9/11 at the request of agency management and in light of contingency planning for USAID's role in the Iraq reconstruction program. This program would eventually become the largest development and reconstruction program ever undertaken by USAID.

I arrived in Kuwait in early November 2002 to interface with the U.S. military in Kuwait, scout for office space and other facilities for USAID, and develop relationships with other organizations (UNDP, WFP, etc.) with which we would likely need to work and coordinate. As far as I know, I was the first American civilian official to deploy to theater, and certainly was the first USAID employee there.

In the meantime, USAID in Washington was beginning to conceive what a post-conflict USAID program would look like and draft scopes of work that would eventually become contracts and grants for work in all the necessary response sectors, such as infrastructure, health, education, community development, economic governance, and local governance. USAID management tried to coordinate our planning with other U.S. Government departments and agencies to some extent.

Overall, however, I recall at this point a total lack of coordinated planning within the U.S. Government for post-conflict Iraq, though we were all at least aware of the State Department's "Future of Iraq Project," led by Tom Warrick. USAID fought for a voice at the so-called Deputies Committee in late 2002.

In late December 2002, I was deployed by USAID Washington to proceed to Qatar to meet with Jay Garner, soon to be head of the Office of Reconstruction and Humanitarian Assistance (ORHA), to discuss early post-conflict planning. While there, we met with CENTCOM Deputy Commander General John Abizaid and discussed plans and progress to date, lessons learned from other conflicts, the need for rapid response, etc.

In January 2003, ORHA was formed and I was recalled to join the organization in Washington as Jay Garner's Deputy for Reconstruction. Apparently some seven previous candidates for the post had been rejected by DOD. I had good rapport with General Garner and liked him from the start.

ORHA was formed by a Presidential Directive that was clearly a DOD product. The directive described ORHA's role and assigned the leadership of each sector of post-conflict reconstruction to a corresponding U.S. Government department: health to the Department of Health and Human Services, education to the Department of Education, trade to the Department of Commerce, and so forth. This key document made no mention of USAID—the U.S. Government's lead economic development and humanitarian response agency.

Thus began what was to become increasingly an OSD-led and directed initiative that was ignorant or dismissive of other parts of the U.S. Government, including the Department of State and USAID—a blatant power grab by OSD to the detriment of the overall U.S. effort.

ORHA assembled in the Pentagon. USAID hurried to identify and hire core mission staff to oversee our Iraq programs. We relied on a personnel contract in place with a Washington-based firm, International Resources Group (IRG), to quickly fill gaps that should have been filled by USAID's own staff—had they been available in sufficient quantity. In my view, ORHA was in chaos at the Pentagon, with little progress being made on office space, other logistics needs, and procedures. I decided I would be more useful helping set up the operation in Kuwait City and departed Washington with the full blessing of Jay Garner and USAID.

Upon arrival in Kuwait I secured USAID's office space and lodging, met with advance teams from the Office of Foreign Disaster Assistance (OFDA), USAID's humanitarian/disaster response branch, and initiated coordination with relevant U.S. military and Kuwaiti officials in preparation for ORHA's arrival in Kuwait City airport by chartered aircraft in late January 2003.

The next 3 months were spent in various training drills, meetings, bio-chem preparations, and office moves. USAID prepared staff as much as we could for management and oversight of our contracts, especially the Bechtel contract—USAID's largest ever, and the key contract for our part of infrastructure repair, which included port, airports, water treatment and conveyance, electricity, bridges, telecommunications, and schools. One early objective for Bechtel was to secure a dredger for the Umm Qasr port, which would be key to the docking of ships carrying food and other essential supplies in case of a humanitarian disaster. The equipment arrived at Umm Qasr from Dubai in time to dredge the port area.

When hostilities began in March 2003, we continued planning and preparations as best we could. We drilled down to who among our staff would enter Baghdad in the first wave and who would follow later. Lack of connectivity kept contracting staff in Kuwait well into June 2003; they would not have been able to function from Baghdad.

Though part of USAID, OFDA was not in my chain of command. OFDA staff in Kuwait did not consider themselves to be under the auspices of ORHA, either. They refused to attend ORHA meetings and resisted cooperation with Garner and other ORHA officials. This rupture was entirely wasteful and unnecessary, and pointed to many future interagency clashes and turf battles that would emerge. This particular battle with OFDA soon surfaced in Washington at the levels of the Secretaries of Defense and State.

It was clear from the start that the entire post-conflict reconstruction program was inadequately planned and inadequately staffed. Even with the best of intentions, and despite the fact that USAID was planning contracts, (ordering armored vehicles, mobilizing staff, etc.) as early as November 2002, in my view no part of the U.S. Government was remotely prepared to implement a well-oiled and coordinated post-conflict reconstruction program. Problems caused by lack of time and preparation were compounded by DOD's "seize the turf" attitude and the apparent neutering of the Department of State and, by extension, its smaller development agency, USAID.

On the infrastructure side, we grossly underestimated the degraded state of Iraqi electricity plants, the port of Umm Qasr, water treatment plants, and sewerage treatment (there was none in Baghdad), and, therefore, the cost and the time required to restore infrastructure. It is worth repeating that, with the exception of the telecommunications sector and three highway bridges, little of the infrastructure damage had been caused by the invasion. Rather, it was the result of lack of maintenance. No one had known the extent of neglect by the Saddam regime and its impact on the state of Iraqi infrastructure. This underestimation was a significant factor regarding timing and expense, but we simply did not have access to better information.

I arrived in Baghdad on April 23, 2003, with two other ORHA deputies, Michael Mobbs and George Ward, and rejoined Jay Garner. The Republican Palace, our new home, was devoid of everything except heat, dust, and a mosaic of Saddam Hussein on the wall. I stayed in Baghdad while ORHA transitioned to CPA. Once a USAID Mission was formally established, I assumed the role of USAID Mission Director. By the end of 2003, USAID had about 130 core staff, including our first Iraqi Foreign Service Nationals (locally hired, non-U.S. employees of USAID), 12 or so large contracts or grants employing hundreds more U.S. and local staff worth about $2 billion at the time, and an increasingly robust, expensive, and necessary security staff.

I departed Baghdad in February 2004 after 15 months in theater with a development and humanitarian program that covered all of Iraq at a cost of some $4 billion and had tallied thousands of successes and accomplishments: thousands of repaid microfinance loans, children vaccinated, schools refurbished, new text books published, health care systems restored, airports and Umm Qasr port fixed and functioning, other infrastructure up and running, hundreds of participatory community development projects completed—all to the credit of our good and courageous U.S. and Iraqi staff, contractors, and grantees. Only a few of these accomplishments received much attention in the press. Apparently this kind of news does not sell newspapers or generate much interest from TV networks.

None of my extended staff was killed or injured during my tenure there, thanks to armored cars, good security procedures, attention to detail, and an excellent USAID Deputy Director, Earl Gast, who oversaw security and security personnel. Regarding security in the face of a growing insurgency, we did our best to be prepared. At times we were just plain lucky.

Based on this experience, I would like to offer two conclusions.

Conclusion One

We were inadequately prepared for the post-conflict stage in Iraq. Others have discussed this point at length, so I will not belabor it. The following are related recommendations, plus discussion, and additional anecdotes from my experience.

Develop, staff, and adequately fund a civilian reconstruction surge capacity. Establishment of S/CRS was a good first step but will not work without adequate permanent staff, excellent recruitment, and followup with volunteers who cover the spectrum of reconstruction/stabilization needs and funding. An enhanced, enlarged, and empowered USAID should have the lead, along with the State Department. DOD should do what DOD does best, and that does not mean leadership on reconstruction. USAID was strapped from the start trying to recruit staff to fill key positions. There are or were no civilian "civil affairs divisions" we could mobilize.

Alternatively, if the U.S. is serious about the "three Ds" of defense, diplomacy and development, for once strengthen the diplomatic and development legs of the stool with adequate staff and funding. USAID can be a great and essential organization in this post-9/11 world, but it cannot run on ether.

Teach project management and U.S. Government contracting rules and procedures to U.S. agencies participating in post-conflict reconstruction. CPA was full of many well-meaning people with no knowledge whatsoever of U.S. Government contract regulations and accountability, which by law must be followed.

Teach next-conflict responders that a complex, government-run reconstruction effort will succeed only if there is a collaborative, "one team" approach and mindset established from the top. This was not the case in Iraq. DOD seized the turf and then did not know what to do with it. Interagency fights were common and preventable. Many true experts from the State Department and USAID (some of whom would return after CPA was abolished to fill key U.S. Embassy positions) were marginalized.

I was a career USAID officer with service in ten countries in Africa, Latin America, and the Middle East for over 28 years. If I were asked which of the various governments I worked with around the world was the most difficult to deal with, the answer would be clear: the United States Government in Iraq was by far the worst, most complex, anti-collaborative, and in too many cases, ineffective one—and I served in West Africa for 8 years. Here are just a few examples of the problems we encountered.

CPA management wanted to control all money, including that of USAID, which had major ongoing projects because of its separate appropriation and comparatively early planning and contracting start—in stark contrast to most other parts of CPA.

CPA appointed a retired U.S. Navy Rear Admiral with no development experience whatsoever to reformulate the overall CPA program budget, including USAID's, for the 2003 supplemental appropriation. In place of an ongoing USAID health program, this official proudly told me he "had taken care of the health program." The solution? He had budgeted, he said, for six garbage trucks for Iraq—a positively preposterous notion, but not atypical of the kind of challenges and, frankly, idiocy we were continuously confronted with. When I protested this decision to highest CPA management, I was told that I was about to have USAID's money "taken away and distributed by CPA in the streets of Hillah." That outburst, in the presence of senior project contractor staff (several retired USAID mission directors, and as capable a bunch as I could ever hope for), led to their wholesale resignation, withdrawn only when the CPA official apologized the next day.

As a corollary to teaching a collaborative approach, recruit staff in key positions who have the minimum required qualifications—rarely the case in CPA, except for such professional organizations as the Department of Treasury, USAID, and the U.S. Army Corps of Engineers—and keep them in place for at least a year. By the time we converted new arrivals to effective allies and friends, they were gone, sometimes after only 3 months. They were replaced by another new crew with whom we had to start all over again.

Conclusion Two

CPA lacked the organizational structure, coherence, experience, leadership, and qualified staffing to carry out its mission effectively. Based on my experience, I would recommend the following.

Develop, recruit, and vet a reconstruction and post-conflict roster of skilled professionals who are willing and able to be deployed quickly in future post-conflict situations. I know this has been started with S/CRS, but with so few staff and such meager resources provided to it so far (and a website for registration that does not work), it is not reassuring.

Hire the right people to do post-conflict reconstruction work. Match personnel with qualifications, regional experience, and, if possible, language skills with the full range of skill sets necessary in future conflicts—local government, microcredit, primary health care, community development, water management, etc. Hire skilled development officials (retirees from USAID, NGOs, private companies, etc.) as leaders in managing this initiative. Keep the roster current and useful.

Organize the umbrella organization that manages reconstruction in a way that is coherent and includes all relevant actors.

Treat coworkers in other agencies as allies, not enemies. Spread the notion that we are all on the same side. This principle is not rocket science, but it was missing in CPA.

When specialists and sector experts are identified and hired, assure them input and access to decisionmakers and help them perform as agents of change. Be careful not to simply allow reconstitution of the former organizational structure (in the case of Iraq, very centralized, top-down decisionmaking) in place of newer, better structures. This is related to the "not prepared" discussion above, and the ad hoc way CPA tried to recruit and manage its way forward. The Iraqis told me CPA stood for "Can't Provide Anything," and at times they were correct.

Leadership of CPA was at times ineffective, poorly informed and poorly advised. To be fair, this was a tough job with overlapping authorities in the midst of a conflict situation, and with the stress of making a hundred major decisions a day. One example of being poorly advised—though the matter was "not in my lane," as the military would say—was the abolition of the Iraqi Army. Why anyone would decide to turn more than one million armed ex-soldiers into the street with their weapons, effectively swelling the ranks of the insurgency, when they otherwise could have been paid to "work for the reconstruction of their country as allies" (as Jay Garner told me) is frankly inexplicable. I have read the rationale offered by the former head of CPA and one of his key advisors at the time. They were dead wrong, and shockingly so.

The same CPA advisor went to the Kurdish region and told the CPA official in charge there that he "needed to demobilize the Peshmerga" (the Kurdish defense force), a wild recommendation that the regional CPA official, an experienced veteran, chose to ignore.

An example of bad leadership was CPA's daily senior staff meeting at 7:00 AM, which devolved into a one-man show (some called it "the shooting gallery"), because agency heads grew tired of being yelled at when they dared to speak up at the meeting. It became clear to me that, to protect and implement our programs, it was crucial to not tell CPA leadership what we were doing. I was not the only one who came to that conclusion.

CPA was also unfortunately populated with inexperienced and very junior staff whose qualifications were not readily apparent. One 24-year-old American working in a key ministry position told me his prior job had been stuffing envelopes in Wisconsin for the 2000 political campaign. We could have done better, and must do so next time.

USAID hired a number of dedicated and qualified contractors who were truly experts—skilled, world-class people who were determined to serve in Iraq, often at a considerable sacrifice of income and security. Yet, CPA sometimes marginalized their contributions by re-instituting the top-down, centralized structure imposed by the former regime. For example, our well-staffed and well-run local governance program was frustrated by lack of access to and support from CPA and ministry officials.

I remain an optimist about Iraq and am putting my money and my feet where my mouth is. I have two companies of my own currently operating in Iraq, one trying to attract American investment into Iraq's petroleum and infrastructure sector, and another building schools. I spend considerable time there.

Iraq is these days a place of increasing stability and opportunity. I continue to believe that Iraq will "make it" because of its resources and the hard work and skills of its people. When they do actually make it, most of the credit will be theirs. I know we, the United States and our coalition partners, despite everything, will have successfully assisted these good people in many ways.

It is incumbent upon us as Americans that we adequately prepare for post-conflict situations such as occurred in Iraq and learn from past mistakes and experience.

Essay 13

Effective Civilian-Military Planning at the Operational Level: The Foundation of Operational Planning

By H.R. McMaster

One of the most important lessons of the war in Iraq is that achieving an outcome consistent with U.S. interests demands effective interdepartmental and multinational planning at the operational level. Although it is clear that decentralization is an essential feature of effective counterinsurgency operations, success at the tactical level, if not connected to well-designed operational plans and a fundamentally sound strategy, is unlikely to be sustained. Moreover, junior leaders and soldiers must understand how their actions fit into the overall plan to defeat the enemy and accomplish the mission. Defeating insurgent organizations and addressing the fundamental causes of violence require a comprehensive approach that must be visualized, described, and directed by an operational commander. Commanders at the operational level—that is, the level of war that "links the tactical employment of forces to national and military and strategic objectives" through the integration of "ends, conditions, ways, and means"—must prioritize efforts and integrate them to achieve clearly defined goals and objectives.[1] Clear operational objectives and plans help ensure that the full range of activities and

---

[1] Joint Publication 3.0, *Joint Operations* (Washington, DC: Department of the Army, September 17, 2006), xiii, xx, available at <http://www.dtic.mil/doctrine/jel/new_pubs/jp3_0.pdf >.

programs are consistent with and contribute to the achievement of policy goals. Sound and continuously revised operational plans are also essential to ensure consistency of effort among units, between military organizations and civil military teams, and over time as the mission progresses.

In addition to integrating the efforts of subordinate organizations, operational commanders and senior civilian officials must also help ensure consistency of effort within multinational coalitions and the interdepartmental, civilian-military team. While an integrated interdepartmental effort in Washington will help in that respect, working together as an integrated team at the operational level is vital. A campaign plan that is understood and accepted by all members of the multinational, civilian-military team is the foundation for achieving unity of effort. The U.S. Army Counterinsurgency field manual emphasizes the importance of integrated civilian-military operational design:

> Through design commanders gain an understanding of the problem and the COIN operation's purpose within the strategic context. Communicating this understanding of the problem, purpose, and context to subordinates allows them to exercise subordinates' initiative. … While traditional aspects of campaign design as expressed in joint and Service doctrine remain relevant, they are not adequate for a discussion of the broader design construct for a COIN environment. Inherent in this construct is the tension created by understanding that military capabilities provide only one component of an overall approach to a COIN campaign. Design of a COIN campaign must be viewed holistically. Only a comprehensive approach employing all relevant design components, including the other instruments of national power, is likely to reach the desired end state.[2]

The military commander and the senior civilian official must form interdepartmental, civilian-military planning teams. Planners must have relevant expertise, knowledge of the situation, and the seniority and

---

[2] Field Manual 3-24 *Counterinsurgency* (Washington, DC: Department of the Army, December 2006), available at <http://www.usgcoin.org/library/doctrine/COIN-FM3-24.pdf>., 4-4.

authority to speak for their departments.[3] When possible, the planning team should include representatives of the supported government, including its security forces. If political sensitivities do not permit their direct participation, it will be essential to consult government representatives to ensure that the operational plan will help achieve unity of effort with the supported government.

Operational design begins with the commander and the senior civilian official deriving their mission and operational goals from policy guidance. A solid connection between policy and operational plans is critical to ensuring that plans are relevant and sufficient resources are available to accomplish the mission. Armed with an understanding of what is to be achieved, the commander and senior civilian official should use their planning team to help them understand the nature of the conflict.

Senior commanders and civilian officials must ask first-order questions to ensure that plans and efforts are feasible and appropriate. Inquiry might begin with an effort to identify and describe the causes of violence. Fundamental causes might include grievances or fears, actions of malign external actors (e.g., hostile states or transnational terrorist organizations), the weakness of the government, and communal competition for power and resources. Ultimately, operational design must address fundamental causes of violence if operational plans are to be effective. If operational design is inconsistent with policy or the nature of the conflict, planning is likely to be driven by what planners might like to do, such as minimize the number of forces committed, avoid difficult state-building tasks, or transition rapidly to indigenous government and security forces that are unprepared to assume full responsibility for security and critical government functions.

Because counterinsurgency operations are inherently complex and uncertain, planning will be based on assumptions. Planners at the operational level must identify assumptions explicitly and ensure that they are logical, essential to the plan, and realistic. If assumptions critical to the success of the plan are unrealistic, the plan is likely to have no effect, or do more harm than good. As the conflict evolves,

---

[3] Areas of expertise include intelligence, security, security sector reform, diplomacy, international development, public finance, economics, reconstruction, rule of law, and governance.

commanders and their staffs must continue to reexamine assumptions, and adjust the plan if events or conditions invalidate them.

An accurate, comprehensive, and constantly revised intelligence estimate is the foundation for planning. Intelligence efforts at the operational level must place the military situation in the context of the political, social, and economic dynamics that are shaping events. The vast majority of intelligence in counterinsurgency comes from below, and from human, rather than technical sources. Although some believe that operational net assessment and other information-based processes can deliver a "system of systems" understanding of the situation, intelligence that is not placed in nuanced political, historical, social, and cultural context, and is not subjected to expert analysis, is useful only for targeting the enemy, and not for understanding the dynamics that are most critical in shaping the outcome of the conflict. Whenever possible, those charged with developing plans at the operational level should travel to sub-regions within the country to gain a detailed understanding of the enemy and political, economic, and social dynamics at the local level. Visits should include meetings with local government officials, tribal or community leaders, and security force leaders. Planning teams must include military and civilian officials with deep historical and cultural knowledge of the country and the region.

After developing the mission and broad objectives, and armed with a comprehensive intelligence estimate, operational planners assist the commander and the senior civilian official in developing the operational logic that will underpin the effort. The operational logic is communicated in the form of *commander's intent*[4] and the *concept of operations*.[5] The commanders' intent describes the broad purpose of operations and identifies key objectives that must be accomplished to ensure mission success. The concept of operations may be the most

---

[4] "A concise expression of the purpose of the operation and the desired end state. It may also include the commander's assessment of the adversary commander's intent and an assessment of where and how much risk is acceptable during the operation," DOD Dictionary, available at <http://www.dtic.mil/doctrine/jel/doddict/data/c/11499 html>.

[5] "A verbal or graphic statement that clearly and concisely expresses what the joint force commander intends to accomplish and how it will be done using available resources. The concept is designed to give an overall picture of the operation. Also called commander's concept or CONOPS," DOD Dictionary, available at <http://www.dtic.mil/doctrine/jel/doddict/data/c/3316 html>.

important part of an operational plan, because it describes to military and civilian leaders how they will combine their own efforts and coordinate those efforts with the partner government to accomplish the mission. The concept describes how the operational commander and senior civilian official see the effort developing over time based on the actions and programs they initiate, as well as the anticipated interaction of those actions and programs with the enemy and other sources of instability. A sound concept is essential for allowing subordinate units and civilian-military teams to take initiative. Moreover, a commonly understood concept serves as a foundation on which planners can develop detailed plans in critical focus areas, or along what are now commonly called "lines of effort," while ensuring that those plans are consistent with the overall concept and are mutually reinforcing.

The Essential Elements of Operational Plans

Because an insurgency is fundamentally a political problem, the foundation for detailed counterinsurgency planning must be a political strategy that drives all other initiatives, actions, and programs. The general objective of the political strategy is to remove or reduce significantly the political basis for violence. The strategy must be consistent with the nature of the conflict, and is likely to address fears, grievances, and interests that motivate organizations within communities to provide active or tacit support for insurgents. Ultimately, the political strategy must endeavor to convince leaders of reconcilable armed groups that they can best protect and advance their interests through political participation, rather than violence.

The political strategy must also foster and maintain a high degree of unity of effort between the supported government and the foreign forces and civilian authorities supporting them. Unity of effort depends, in part, on a common understanding of the nature of the conflict, definition of the problem set, and agreement on the broad approach necessary to defeat insurgent organizations and achieve sustainable security. If the indigenous government pursues policies or takes actions that exacerbate rather than ameliorate the causes of violence, the political strategy must address how to influence the government by demonstrating that an alternative approach is necessary to avert defeat and achieve an outcome consistent with its interests. If institutions or functions of the supported state are captured by malign or corrupt organizations that pursue agendas inconsistent with the political strategy, it may become necessary to employ a range of cooperative, persuasive, and coercive means to reverse that situation and restore a cooperative relationship.

The military component of operational plans must be derived from and support the political strategy. The concept for military operations must be grounded in the intelligence estimate. Planners must understand the nature and structure of enemy organizations, their ideology or political philosophy, the strategy that they are pursuing, their sources of strength, and their vulnerabilities. At a high level of generalization, operations should aim to isolate enemy organizations from sources of strength while attacking enemy vulnerabilities in the physical, political, informational, and psychological domains. Defeating the insurgents' campaign of intimidation and coercion through effective population security is a necessary precondition for achieving political progress and gaining the intelligence necessary to conduct effective offensive operations. Military forces pursue "irreconcilables" not only to defeat the most committed and dangerous enemy organizations, but also to convince "reconcilables" to commit to a political resolution of the conflict.

Operational plans must integrate reform of the indigenous government's security agencies and the development of capable and legitimate security forces into the overall security effort. To defeat an insurgency or end a communal struggle associated with an insurgency, people must trust their own government and security forces to fulfill their most basic need—security. While local military units and civilian-military teams focus on training and operating alongside indigenous police and Army units, senior commanders, civilian officials, and their staffs should focus on building the administrative capacity and professionalism of security ministries. Senior commanders must work with the host government to craft a plan for the development of ministerial capacity that is grounded in a common understanding of security force roles and missions, and the force structure necessary to perform those roles and missions. The plan must be long-term. Plans must initiate work on systems and capabilities that take time to mature, such as leader development, public financial management, personnel management, logistics, and infrastructure. Because indigenous forces will ultimately be responsible for maintaining security, security force capability and capacity must be sufficient to maintain security after foreign supporting forces depart.

Identifying and developing capable leaders who are committed to improving the security of all citizens rather than advancing a particularistic agenda or personal interests may be the most critical requirement. Because a lack of trust and confidence in security forces often fuels an insurgency, particular attention must be paid to the loyalty and professionalism of those forces (e.g., through leader development and thorough screening of recruits), and a sustained effort must be made to mediate between those forces and their own populations to build confidence. Because all insurgencies include a dimension of civil conflict, it is important that operational planning for security sector reform be closely integrated with the political strategy and ensure that security forces are generally representative of the population and contribute to improved security rather than to conflict between communities competing with one another. Operational plans must also emphasize fostering cooperation between indigenous military forces, police forces, and intelligence services.

The integration of reconstruction and economic development into security operations is critical to rekindling hope among the population and demonstrating that tangible benefits will flow from sustained cooperation with counterinsurgent forces. Local commanders and civilian-military teams need access to funds and development expertise. Technical assistance should put indigenous systems and leaders at the center of the effort and focus on such critical functions as public financial management. Programs that initiate sustainable economic growth and employment, such as agricultural programs and microloans and medium-size loan programs, are particularly valuable. Operational-level plans should identify and advance macroeconomic policies that remove obstacles to economic growth (e.g., legal impediments to foreign direct investment, and subsidies that provide a disincentive to entrepreneurship or incentivize corruption) and provide a stable economic environment (e.g., low inflation). Plans should also account for international and non-governmental organizations' development programs to reduce redundancies and identify opportunities for collaboration and burden-sharing. If improvements in this area are to be sustained, local efforts must be recognized by and connected to governmental institutions. For example, an effort to build clinics at the local level will fail without ensuring that the health ministry hires health care providers and funds maintenance of the facility in its operational budget. Similarly, efforts to improve governance and law enforcement at the local level must be tied to efforts at the provincial and national levels. Despite the best efforts to improve security and move communities toward political accommodation, the pool of popular discontent from which an insurgency draws strength will grow if local government is ineffective.

Because establishing the rule of law is a particularly important element of effective counterinsurgency operations, it must receive focused attention from military and civilian officials at the operational level. Senior commanders and civilian authorities must work with indigenous government personnel to help establish a legal framework that allows the government to defeat the insurgency while protecting basic human rights. Because effective rule of law poses a threat to the insurgent organization, insurgents will seek to intimidate police and judges. Counterinsurgents, therefore, must protect as well as build police investigative and judicial capacity. Until security conditions permit the normal functioning of the judicial system, government and counterinsurgency forces may have to develop a transparent, review-based detainee system that ensures humane treatment. While it is important to ensure that innocents are not imprisoned, it is also important to keep committed insurgents behind bars. As David Galula observed, if the counterinsurgent releases insurgents back into a violent environment, "the effects will soon be felt by the policeman, the civil servant, and the soldier."[6] Because detention facilities are critical battlegrounds, it is important to assist the supported government in extending counterinsurgency efforts into those facilities. Important measures include the segregation of leaders, intelligence collection, and rehabilitation prior to release and reintegration.

Operational level commanders, civil authorities, and the local government must infuse all of their activities with effective communications to relevant audiences, especially the indigenous population and the leaders of the supported government and security forces. Critical tasks include clarifying the counterinsurgents' intentions, countering enemy disinformation and propaganda, and bolstering the legitimacy of the government and its security forces. It is also important to trace the population's grievances back to the enemy while exposing the enemy's brutality and indifference to the welfare of

---

[6] David Galula, *Counterinsurgency Warfare: Theory and Practice* (Westport, CT: Praeger Security International, 1964), 62.

the population. Operational plans must connect themes and messages to appropriate media platforms and establish a means of assessing how communications are perceived by the population. Decentralization is critical, because local political and cultural dynamics (and their associated messages) will vary considerably. Senior commanders and civil authorities must, however, provide guidance such that local efforts in this area are mutually reinforcing.

Operational planning must also develop an "external solution" to complement the counterinsurgency effort inside the country. Diplomatic, economic, and international law enforcement efforts are necessary to help isolate insurgent organizations from external support. In general, diplomatic efforts should aim to integrate the supported government into the region and enlist the support of reluctant or uncommitted neighbors. Diplomatic or military efforts might also be necessary to convince malign regional actors to desist from activities that undermine the effort.

Once the plan is framed and broadly consistent with the nature of the conflict and the situation, it is important to identify long-term, intermediate, and near-term goals in each focus area and identify the key tasks, programs, and actions necessary to achieve those goals over time. Planners and analysts should identify obstacles to progress in each focus area and propose how to overcome those obstacles. Plans must identify and allocate the resources necessary to accomplish tasks and affix clear responsibility for accomplishing them. Near-term goals should contribute to the first priority of achieving sustainable security and stability. Longer-term goals should aim to help transform the society such that the fundamental causes of violence are dramatically reduced. Ideally, actions and programs undertaken in the near term build toward achieving long-term goals. While it is important to keep long-term objectives in mind, it is also important to understand that there may be no long term if the supported government is unable to achieve visible progress and gain the trust of the population. Critical, long-term efforts, such as civil service reform, the implementation of anticorruption measures, establishment of the rule of law, and the development of leaders in the security sector must be initiated early if adequate progress is to be made in time to stabilize the situation.

Continuous Reassessment

It is difficult to overstate the importance of constant reassessment. The nature of a conflict will continue to evolve because of continuous interaction with enemies and other destabilizing factors. Progress will never be linear, and there will have to be constant refinements and readjustments to even the best plans. Commanders and senior civilian officials should be aware that overreliance on systems analysis can create an illusion of control and progress. Metrics often tell commanders and civilian officials how they are executing their plan (e.g., money spent, numbers of indigenous forces trained and equipped, districts or provinces transferred to indigenous control), but fail to highlight logical disconnects. Estimates of the situation often underestimate the enemy and other sources of instability. These estimates, in turn, serve as a foundation for plans that are inconsistent with the nature of the conflict. An overreliance on metrics can lead to a tendency to develop short-term solutions for long-term problems and a focus on simplistic charts rather than on deliberate examinations of questions and issues critical to the war effort. Moreover, because of wide variations in conditions at the local level, much of the data that is aggregated at the national level is of little utility.

Lessons Learned in Democratic Transition and Building Civil Society

By William Montgomery

I was privileged to be present and, to some extent, a participant, in the downfall of Communist rule in Bulgaria in 1990–91, the end of the authoritarian government of the Croatian Democratic Union in 1999–2000, and the electoral defeat of Slobodan Milosevic and his subsequent arrest and extradition to the International Criminal Tribunal for the Former Yugoslavia in The Hague in 2000–2001. All three of these cases attracted wide media attention, and all were celebrated as major steps forward by Western powers.

The most important lesson I learned from these experiences is that they shouldn't be seen as the happy endings we Americans love in our movies, when the oppressed democrats overcome persecution and live happily ever after. Instead, these events are merely the end of one chapter in a country's history and the beginning of another. Bringing down authoritarian rulers is comparatively simple in comparison with the follow-on work of accomplishing a democratic transition and establishing a competitive, market-oriented economy. The less historical experience the countries have with these concepts, the harder the task will be, and the longer it will take.

In these three cases, there was a complex web of beliefs, prejudices, ingrained practices, and historical experience in place that conflicted with Western values and practices. Transforming these societies is a challenge spanning generations. In each instance it was particularly difficult to bring change to academia, the security services, and the judiciary. One still finds professors in state universities teaching economics who held the same posts in the Communist era. Senior intelligence personnel are still in place from the earlier eras, and still view their primary task as monitoring the local population; the new, "democratic" political leaders are discouragingly pleased with the information these operatives convey. Many of the most senior judges came up through the former Communist system and still feel that it is their responsibility, or is in their personal interest, to support the system in power rather than the rule of law. Overriding all of the above is ingrained corruption that touches all levels of society. In fact, it is a bigger problem now than 10 years ago.

Despite billions of dollars of assistance, advisors of all kinds, and consistent pressure to change, we have in most cases only been able to have a marginal impact on this process. Clearly it will take far longer than a generation to complete under the best of circumstances. When analyzing the problem, one should think about American attitudes in the 1950s on such issues as smoking, the environment, civil rights, and gay rights. We have made great progress in each of these areas, but it has taken us 50 years and a lot of pain and controversy to do so. Moreover, all of these issues remain alive today. We need to see the process of democratic transformation in exactly the same way, in exactly the same sort of time-frame.

The second lesson is related to the first. President Obama recently described his Iraq policy by saying, "We will not let the perfect get in the way of the achievable." This is a huge, costly lesson learned from the battlefields of Iraq and Afghanistan. I only hope we keep it mind when considering future interventions. We certainly did not apply it to the Balkans. Bosnia is a classic example. Out of a combination of principle and naiveté, we forged our policy on the pillars of "no change in the borders of Bosnia through use of force" and rebuilding a fully functioning, multi-ethnic society in that war-scarred country. It's hard to argue against either of those goals. Even now, 15 years after the Dayton Agreement, doing so will bring down a hailstorm of criticism from almost every expert in the U.S. foreign policy establishment.

The reality is, however, that we have spent billions of dollars in resources, treated Bosnia as one of our major foreign policy priorities for the 8 years of the Clinton Administration, and have maintained a huge international presence there for 15 years now—and there is no end in sight. Bosnia remains at best a second-class country on the fringes of

Europe. Senior officials such as Richard Holbrooke and Paddy Ashdown have sounded the alarm in recent editorials that Bosnia risks sliding backward toward its violent past.

The reason is simple: the international community is insisting on pounding a square peg (a multi-ethnic, fully functioning Bosnia with no border changes) into a round hole. I know this full well: I was one of the main "pounders" for a lot of my diplomatic career. The three ethnic parties have never abandoned their prewar goals, assumptions, fears, suspicions, and hostilities toward each other. If anything, the war sharpened them. Forget all the figures and other measures of success advanced by those trying to put a positive face on our policy approach. Look at the percentage of multi-ethnic marriages. In the prewar period it was over 20 percent. Now it is zero.

The Dayton Agreement put in place a constitution and a system of government that was, to recast President Obama's words, "perfect but not achievable." The agreement contains a fundamental inconsistency: it created two entities and gave each of them a great deal of autonomy—so much autonomy that the central government was impossibly weak. Moreover, all three ethnic groups were given countless safeguards and veto power over anything that could remotely be conceived as threatening their "national interests."

The end result is that the Bosniaks want to have the International Community abolish the Republika Srpska altogether, or at least take away a lot of its autonomy. The Bosnian Croats look to Croatia in terms of dual citizenship, education, and employment. The Bosnian Serbs don't even consider themselves to be Bosnians, but citizens of the Republika Srpska. These factors constantly prevent real cooperation or interaction between the entities or the three ethnic groups. The UN, recognizing the dangers of a reversion to violence, keeps extending the mandate of its High Representative. Bosnia remains a backwater: poor, unstable, an exporter of young people seeking better lives, a festering crisis waiting to happen. And all because we are insisting, as we have for 15 years, on the perfect and not simply the achievable.

The third, hard-won lesson is that for the process of democratic transition to have a chance to succeed where fighting or widespread violence has occurred, intensive cooperation is required between our military and civilian components. The initial phase of the Balkan experience was not good. In 1996 and most of 1997, the U.S. military in Bosnia adamantly refused to participate in what they considered civilian activities. They saw their role as providing basic security. They went so far as to refuse to apprehend indicted war criminals such as Mladic and Karadzic, who traveled with ease through our checkpoints, gave TV interviews on the ski slopes of Jahorina, and attended political rallies with impunity. The military actually opposed return of refugees to places where they would be the ethnic minority on the grounds that their return could cause conflict.

The fault wasn't only on one side. At the time, each military unit had a certain amount of funding for civic action programs in its area of responsibility, and civic action experts to carry out these tasks. They concentrated on small-scale projects such as repairing a small bridge and putting a roof on a school. The idea was to win over the local population. When they approached USAID for additional funding for these projects, they were rudely rejected. USAID had its own priorities and was not even civil in brushing off the assistance requests.

Judging from reports from Iraq and Afghanistan, we have learned that we need to work together. But a lot more must be done. The State Department, in particular, needs to be greatly expanded and its personnel given extensive training in building civil society. That is not done now—it is all learning on the job. Furthermore, the fundamental shortage of Foreign Service Officers means that, in times of need, the Foreign Service cannot respond without gutting its other responsibilities. So, time and again, our government is forced to turn to the military to do tasks that should fall on the civilian side. The military has the personnel and resources, which the State Department lacks. Secretary of Defense Gates' recent efforts to convince Congress of the need for greater State Department resources and personnel are encouraging, and indeed in DOD's institutional interest.

A start on improving this whole process would be to design a one-year course on nation-building techniques, similar to the one year courses offered by the National War College, and perhaps offered at National Defense University. An equal number of military and civilian personnel from key agencies would attend, learning to work together based on case studies and practical experience. Not only would this course build expertise, it would create the sort of networking ties for which the National War College is justly renowned. We also need a forum or some organization to look hard at lessons learned to create a basic "bible" on how our agencies will work together and what tasks are the most essential to accomplish to lay the foundations for democratic transition and civil society.

Finally, while the United States may have been—and may still be in the future—the primary outside force attempting to bring about democratic transition and build civil society around the world, it absolutely cannot do the job alone. It needs partners, both like-minded allies and international institutions such as the UN, IMF, World Bank, NATO, and the OSCE. Creating such partnerships has always been a very difficult process, as other countries and institutions have their own agendas and practices, which under the best of circumstances will never be identical to our own.

American influence in this area will decline further as the world continues to shift away from the "American century" and becomes inevitably far more multi-polar. What this means is that the world will become increasingly chaotic and unpredictable while the mechanisms we have for dealing with crises become less reliable and less effective.

The lesson to be learned here is a particularly difficult one for Americans. One of our greatest strengths—and also one of our greatest weaknesses—has been our willingness and determination to take decisive, unilateral action when we believe it necessary. We are impatient and often dismissive when confronted with what we see as obstructionism, bureaucratic delays, or timidity to act. We are going to have to learn an entirely new set of skills: how to work most effectively in this complex web of countries, non-state players, and institutions.

What should be glaringly obvious after Iraq, but also after Kosovo, is that acting unilaterally or with a "coalition of the willing" inevitably makes it much harder to carry out the far more difficult, long-term task of building civil society and democratic practices. We must work much harder to get consensus before we act, and at times grit our teeth and not act, absent consensus. This is the toughest lesson of all.

Striking the Right Balance

By William L. Nash

When asked to reflect on my experiences in dealing with complex operations, most people expect me to discuss my service as a multinational division commander in a peace enforcement mission in Bosnia-Herzegovina in 1995–1996 or my duties as a civil administrator for the United Nations in Kosovo in 2000. But as I look back on my military service and post-retirement work, the place to begin is my experience as a platoon leader in Vietnam in 1969. Also relevant is the immediate aftermath of Operation *Desert Storm* in 1991, when I was an armored brigade commander in southern Iraq.

I had little or no training in humanitarian relief, political-military issues, economic development, or the rule of law—the very subjects that confronted me when I was on operations. With the exception of some counterinsurgency exercises in my pre-Vietnam military experience and in the 4 months before my division's deployment to Bosnia, the United States Government did not address the non-military challenges. We fought battles in our training exercises, where we learned that civilians were something to be kept away. The civil affairs officers and units were charged with handling the civilians; the fighters were not to be bothered while we went about the serious work.

But all was different in the real world. There were civilians everywhere. In Vietnam, we seldom went a day without running into small villages, clusters of thatched huts with women, children and old men present. Many were sympathetic to our enemy, but they were noncombatants, and all too often our hatred or fear of the enemy combatants affected how we behaved toward the noncombatants. We treated few with the dignity and respect that they deserved as fellow humans. We did not realize to the degree necessary that our behavior toward these people could affect our ability to achieve success on the battlefield in the long term. From time to time we did some medical community action program missions, or "MEDCAPs," to provide a modicum of short-term health care, or we pulled security while engineers fixed a road and repaired a bridge, but improving the overall circumstances of the ordinary citizen was not part of a coherent plan. It certainly was not part of a political, economic, and security plan that the soldiers with all the guns understood. It was not that we harmed civilians; we just did not know how important it was to help them. We did not know when to build instead of fight.

In Iraq, I was told by a senior commander not to build a refugee camp for the thousands of Iraqis fleeing Saddam's terror for our area of operations. I told him I could do the job "organized or unorganized," which would he prefer? He then told me, "not to build a permanent one!" For the next two months, we made it up as we went along. Again the strategic plan was unclear to us on the ground until it was time to execute the next action: evacuate the refugees that wanted to leave—prepare for redeployment—no, we need a Post-Desert Storm strategic reserve force, you're it, Nash—go establish a base camp near Kuwait City, and prepare contingency plans.

Militarily, we were much better prepared for the Bosnian mission. The 1st Armored Division had worked a variety of plans since late 1992. The military provisions of the Dayton Accord, though limited, were well thought through with an eye to the practicalities of on-the-ground implementation. So when we deployed in late 1995, the hard part was getting there and setting up a very large footprint of forces throughout the country.

Each of the warring factions had made a strategic decision to stop fighting, so our efforts at enforcement were focused on the specific details of the peace agreement, not the process of stopping the fighting. But it soon became clear that not fighting and peace were two different things. Also, the political and economic aspects of the Dayton Accord were not as precise as the military aspects, and the resources and leadership to implement the civilian aspects were not forthcoming. So we achieved routine, habitual compliance with the military terms of the

Dayton Accord, and over time the force levels were reduced, but the political confrontations and the economic stagnation continued.

Kosovo was my first experience on the other side of the civilian-military line. I was the Regional Civil Administrator in Northern Kosovo, with headquarters in Mitrovica—that is where the Albanian majority in the south changed to a Serb majority in the north at the Ibar River, which ran through the middle of town. This division had an overriding influence on everything we did. Hatred and fear were manifest every day in the eyes and actions of citizens—much worse than in Bosnia. Maintaining law and order was a constant challenge. The organization of KFOR, the UN police, courts and civil authority was not suited for an effective, efficient, or consistent rule of law environment. On the infrastructure and economic front, I had projects, not programs. That meant that while there were many individual projects being implemented by the KFOR, UNDP, USAID, the British DFID, and scores of NGOs, there was no international, national or regional integration authority to bring everything together. Many officials tried to make sense of all these projects, but the results were much less than what was required. The impact was negative because economics affect politics, and vice versa. Therefore, decisions taken by an individual authority, without regard to consequences on other areas or functions meant various actors could work the system by making mutually exclusive promises to serve selfish needs. In the end, state-building requires the integration of political, economic, security, legal, and social actions to create a cohesive whole.

Don't ever forget that *complex operations are about people*. The reasons for intervention may be clouded in self-serving, interests-based, realist politics or even in humanitarian values that seek to right years of wrong, but at the point of action, it's about people.

It's about an 8-year-old Vietnamese boy who shows up to play catch with a Frisbee whenever the Americans come by to get supplies near his home; and it's about the quizzical look on his face when he's presented the Frisbee one day, and everybody in the platoon comes by to shake his hand because we're leaving his area. What happens next?

It's about a soon-to-be refugee who pauses a few minutes to look at the waiting C-130 and the surrounding desert, clearly deciding whether or not he should board the aircraft and leave his native land for an unknowable future. Finally, he sighs and grabs a hand full of sand, thrusting it in his pocket before boarding the plane.

It's about a Croatian Corps commander who strongly objects to a very minor adjustment to the Inter-Entity Boundary Line in Bosnia-Herzegovina, explaining that the 25x50-meter plot taken from his territory was the reason he fought in a 4-year war—it was his grandmother's farm!

It's about two Albanian and Serb leaders who, when allowed to escape the press of events—the constituents who demand extreme political positions, the inquiring press who demand explanations for every past and future action—can sit down, drink a cup of coffee together, and bargain, explain, argue, and agree on steps to achieve some progress on the political and economic issues facing them.

This lesson about people is so important, yet so easy to overlook as events press in on those who are there to lead, command, and manage an intervention. Soldiers have long known how to take care of the troops; now we also need to take care of the people. Customer-based operations are an essential part of what needs to be done. The key question for the population is whether or not their lives are better today and their opportunities are greater than before the intervention.

Everything is related to everything. The hallmark of complex operations is that they are so damned complicated. There are too many players, too many issues, too many problems. Working on and fixing just one problem all too frequently causes troublesome, unintended consequences. Digging a well, and providing fresh water in Southern Iraq is only part of the problem. Who owns the land? Who will control access when U.S. forces move on? Have you just empowered a "warlord" and lessened U.S. credibility? It took me 3 weeks to sort out the business and political issues involved in putting a bus station in Mitrovica. There was no avoiding making both a friend and several enemies with that decision. Transparency in decisionmaking normally helps, but only partially. Empowering the indigenous population is essential, but this is new territory for most, and the quest for power and wealth seldom remains dormant.

The elusive goal is to understand the interrelated nature of the political, economic, social, and security factors. A military-style execution matrix that provides visibility to these elements, even if not perfect, is a start. Getting lots of input from staff, subordinate commanders, and local players is important. Taking the time to find the right people with diverse views to talk to is very important.

There is an understandable tension here with wanting to make progress early on in an operation—the window of opportunity—and taking the time to make sound decisions after considering the myriad of related issues. I would advise focusing fast action on security, humanitarian relief, the provision of basic services (electricity, water, sewage/garbage and basic health care), and road repair. There are dangers here, too, as I earlier noted, but if the population as a whole is served, then missteps can be corrected over time.

Know when to shoot and when to build. I return to an impression from Vietnam about not fully understanding what today is called kinetic vs. non-kinetic solutions. When you're in a fight, there's not much doubt that you must succeed and care for your soldiers. We are very good at that—sometimes too good, in that we tend to overuse firepower. But the larger picture, the Nation's welfare today and tomorrow demands that we be judicious, and be seen not as a force for destruction, but as a force for good in the world.

At the strategic and operational level, we have to be ready to shoot and be building all the time. Even in a fast-paced attack to seize critical objectives, care must be taken to integrate, follow, and support operations that help improve the affected population even if the fight is still ongoing. This is a "walk and chew gum" exercise! There's no alternative. Much has been written of late about how to conduct counterinsurgency operations. The very best counterinsurgency strategy is to avoid the rise of an insurgency by comprehensive planning that looks over time through an intervention and provides for more building than fighting.

The same soldiers who played a major role in the destruction of the Republican Guards in *Desert Storm* built and operated that "temporary" refugee camp I mentioned. There was no special training required; the soldiers were given a reasonable mission, and they got the job done. It could be argued that the longest-lasting contribution of the 1st Armored Division to Bosnia-Herzegovina was the support given to the creation of what has become known as the Arizona Market. The responsible brigade commander noticed that the only place where Serbs, Croats, and Bosniaks ever gathered peacefully was near an American checkpoint. There they bartered food, cigarettes, gasoline, and whatever else they had. Instead of breaking up this congestion on one of our most important military routes, the brigade commander recommended clearing some space off to the side to allow commercial activity to continue. It only took a few truckloads of gravel and willingness to take a bit of risk to get the market started. Today, the Arizona Market is a multi-million dollar, multi-ethnic wholesale/retail complex near the town of Brcko.

The bottom line is that I believe it is very important to understand and accept the complexity of our post-Cold War/post-9/11 operations; organize accordingly, and use all the skills and abilities of our Nation in achieving better conditions for the people we seek to influence. It's their world, too.

Understanding and Responding to Fragile and Failed States

By Andrew S. Natsios

T he U.S government has spent tens of billions of dollars responding to crises in fragile and failed states since the end of the Cold War. What have we learned about the nature of these crises, their internal dynamics, and how best to respond to them given their frequency?

To respond effectively to complex crises we must understand not only the humanitarian aspects that often receive the bulk of our attention, but also the internal political and economic dynamics of the situation.

The most serious mistake made regularly by NGOs, UN agencies, IFIs, and donor aid agencies has been focusing on the purely humanitarian consequences of complex crises without understanding the internal political and economic dynamics that produced them. Cause and consequence should not be conflated. Complex crises are caused by destabilizing political and economic forces, not vice versa. In virtually all such crises, economic forces combine with political dynamics in insidious ways to cause chaos. As Douglass North has pointed out, chaos is a natural tendency of all social orders under stress that do not have strong institutions to bind society together. Most aid agencies conduct rapid humanitarian assessments in the early stages of a crisis to determine needs in four areas so that they may respond appropriately: public health, including water and sanitation; food and nutrition; shelter; and emergency medical care. Western military forces engaged in aid efforts compound this counterproductive tendency by reducing aid programs to logistics operations to move around relief commodities in the case of disaster relief in civil conflicts or infrastructure projects during reconstruction after a conflict.

Instead of focusing only on the humanitarian nature of the crisis, we should be conducting simultaneous analysis to determine the economics of chaos operating in the society: are markets functioning? Why? Who controls them? What are the principal sources of wealth, and who controls them? How do the sources of wealth interact with the forces that are causing the chaos and violence? What populations are at risk of human rights abuses and mass atrocities, and who or what is putting them at risk? Complex crises are nearly all about power and wealth, and who controls them within a social order. Without understanding those dynamics the humanitarian aid effort can unintentionally contribute to spreading chaos instead of relieving it. Stability operations are about *stability*, not only humanitarian aid, and the restoration of equilibrium in a society so that the self-sufficiency of a society can be reestablished as soon as possible.

We experimented with several techniques for determining the dynamics of dissolution at work in societies under severe stress. First, deploying microeconomists with substantial field experience in development work and conflicts to observe local markets in operation over a several-week period can produce hard analysis about the economic forces at work. Market analysis in Somalia in 1992 proved central to our understanding of how looted donor food aid had become the medium of economic exchange and the means for warlords to hire irregular troops and keep discipline in their militias. Observing local arms markets in Bosnia and Somalia in the early 1990s helped us understand the movement of small arms into the conflict zones. We commissioned a survey by university researchers of people in Panama City following the overthrow of Noriega, and of 1,200 people in Afghanistan in early 2002 and in 2004, randomly chosen within six provinces, with each person interviewed for on average 2 hours on their household economic situation, coping mechanisms, and priorities for survival; no political issues were addressed. In the Afghan surveys we found that the severe indebtedness of families accumulated through 5 years of drought and war was damaging the social order and community life, and that water and personal security were the greatest needs and were driving family decisionmaking. These three conclusions in the Afghan surveys helped us redesign our reconstruction strategy to focus more resources on economic growth through agriculture and more funding for water projects, particularly for animal herds and irrigation. Thirdly, we developed a conflict analysis instrument that has been tested in 15 countries and helps us to understand the forces encouraging the dissolution of a society and those forces contributing to its stability. At a minimum, U.S. policy should try to avoid making matters worse (the "do no harm" principle) and try to support and encourage the stabilizing forces in the society. How this is done varies widely from crisis to crisis: local context is essential in undertaking this analysis.

Among the two most destabilizing yet common events in societies in crisis are violence against civilian populations and subsequent mass population movements. Finding out what groups are at risk and why is not easy, and yet it is essential to designing a strategy to prevent or mitigate it if it breaks out. Atrocities inevitably ignite cycles of retributive violence, where survivors of the initial atrocities take revenge on civilians from the groups that committed atrocities against their families. These cycles of violence can complicate reconstruction efforts.

We have found some effective ways of limiting retributive violence. Burundi, a society with the same caste and ethnic cleavages as Rwanda, did not descend into the same sort of blood bath as did Rwanda[1], because religious leaders in Burundi were given access to the public radio stations to broadcast religious messages of peaceful resolution of disputes, non-violence, and forgiveness. Leaders of the Parliament from both ethnic groups walked through community neighborhoods and told people to stay calm and remain in their homes. In other words, carefully planned and quickly implemented public action using high visibility means such as mass media can contain potentially explosive situations. Conversely the infamous radio station, Radio Mille Collines, used the airwaves to organize the atrocities against the Tutsi population and moderate Hutus during the Rwandan genocide. Had the United States (or another western power) blown up or at least jammed the broadcasts of the station, there is a chance the violence could have been limited.

Population movements are among the most socially destructive, economically damaging, and politically destabilizing of any of the consequences of a complex crisis. Disease epidemics spread much more rapidly when populations move en masse, nutritional status

---

[1] The Presidents of Rwanda and Burundi were assassinated together in a plane crash in April 1994 that ignited the genocide in Rwanda.

deteriorates precipitously, economic productivity declines as people usually cannot move their jobs and livelihoods with them, violence against women increases exponentially as the protection of male relatives and community structure evaporates, and property ownership becomes a politicized and divisive issue as other people move in and take abandoned land and homes, causing later legal disputes over ownership. Under international law people cannot be physically prohibited from moving, particularly if they feel threatened, so that option ought not to be considered (it has been ineffective in the past operationally, in any case). Instead, efforts should be made to determine why people are moving, and design a strategy to change the incentives causing the population movements. In Iraq we know that there was a rural-to-urban migration taking place because of the virtual collapse of the rural economy even before U.S. and coalition forces arrived. Some of the young men who moved to urban areas became homeless and hungry on the streets and were recruited into the militias. A rural agricultural development program in Iraq immediately following the U.S. military intervention could have reversed the economic incentives for migration by reviving the rural economy. The CPA refused to fund a $100 million USAID agriculture program in Iraq designed for immediate implementation. This decision was reversed in late 2005, too late to slow the migrations to the cities that later helped to fuel the insurgency.

Another example of what we could have done to change destructive economic dynamics on the ground in a complex crisis took place in Afghanistan. We distributed to Afghan farmers an improved wheat seed variety in early 2002 that was drought resistant and very productive, doubling wheat production per hectare. Combined with the first good rains in 5 years, Afghanistan produced the best wheat crop in its history—so good that wheat prices collapsed to 20 percent of the average yearly price. The price was so depressed that some farmers did not even harvest the wheat and let it rot in their fields. Farmers decided to grow poppy for heroin the next year because it was a more reliable income producer. In the same year, 200,000 MT of U.S. food aid, mostly wheat, was distributed by the World Food Program (WFP) and non-governmental organizations to returning refugees, displaced people, and impoverished families. Federal law requires all U.S. food aid to be purchased in the United States. Had we been able to purchase the food aid locally from the large Afghan wheat surplus we could have stabilized prices and created incentives for farmers to grow more wheat the following year. More flexibility in the U.S. food aid program, which the Bush Administration attempted unsuccessfully to get through Congress (the proposal was to allow up to 25 percent of U.S. food aid under PL 480 to be purchased locally) could have had profound economic consequences for the agricultural system in Afghanistan. With the exception of conflicts in the Balkans, virtually all complex crises over the past 30 years have taken place in countries whose economies were essentially agricultural. Programs to stimulate rural economic growth, reduce food insecurity, implement quick-impact programs to improve agricultural productivity, and their relationship to agricultural markets and pricing systems could yield prompt and powerful results—if food aid could be used to support rather than undermine these programs.

The implementation and coordination of aid programs presents mind-numbing challenges in failing, failed, and recovering states with high levels of insecurity, collapsed or non-existent institutions, and a weak indigenous government. Five international development banks, a half dozen UN specialized agencies, dozens of non-governmental organizations and private for- profit companies, and two dozen donor aid agencies make up an extraordinarily complex international aid architecture for the spending of funds on humanitarian assistance (to save lives) and long-term development and reconstruction. We have learned five management lessons from our experience in a dozen complex crises concerning how we might improve performance of the international aid system.

The first lesson is that while this complex system is not under any central control, it relies on a loose system of voluntary coordination among independent actors that is only effective if there is strong UN and World Bank leadership with a mandate to get aid agencies to share this sort of information and undertake joint strategic planning with the indigenous government (if there is one of any competence). Without competent and strong international leadership, properly staffed through these institutions holding a robust mandate, coordination will fail.

Second, the complexity of the aid system can be reduced by donors placing funds in each other's program implementation mechanisms (if they like what they see) rather than insisting on their own, thus reducing the number of independent management units doing work.

This is being done on a much more regular basis by donor aid agencies than ever before, as internal business systems of aid agencies are being redesigned to allow them to fund each other's programs.

Third, we face serious accountability problems if we put aid funds directly into the local government treasuries through what is called budget support, to fund the new, but weak governments in post-conflict circumstances. We developed several mechanisms to try to get the ownership and buy in of these fledgling governments, and yet ensure accountability. To get Afghan government officials' salaries paid just after the Karzai government was formed in 2002, UNDP set up a salary payroll system under its control, funded with donor government contributions, that was independent of the Afghan government but ensured that every verifiable public employee got paid on a regular basis.

Fourth, to avoid weaknesses in the Afghan government's virtually non-existent procurement system, USAID used its own procurement systems to put contracts in place to improve Afghan government ministries. To get Afghan buy in and ownership in the contracts, competent ministry officials were put on the USAID decisionmaking committees that analyzed the bids and chose winning bidders. This arrangement ensured local ownership and participation, but avoided the corruption in the Afghan government procurement system.

Fifth, when the Afghan rural development ministry put in place a local grants program, the ministry chose a U.S.-based contractor, DAI, as the fiduciary agent for donor funding for the program to make sure money was disbursed using accountable and transparent systems.

These innovations in management did not solve all of the extraordinarily complex management problems in complex crisis response, but they improved the international aid system and ought to be replicated elsewhere.

More sweeping proposals for reform are sometimes proposed in the international aid architecture without realizing the enormous obstacles to change. Embracing an incremental approach that makes small improvements carefully and systematically over time has a higher likelihood of success.

Implementation in a Multiparty Environment

By Ronald E. Neumann

Human relations trump organizational charts and theories of coordination. My experiences in Iraq under the Coalition Provisional Authority (CPA) and as U.S. Ambassador in Afghanistan provide the following examples of the complexity of multi-party environments and some suggestions for action.

You don't know what you don't know, and it's harder to find out what you don't know than you think

A recurring frustration comes when leaders find problems they hadn't known existed. In Afghanistan, decisionmakers agreed on assistance programs only to find out several months later that nothing had moved. "We're having trouble getting consensus in the working group," was a frequent answer.[1] General Karl Eikenberry and I each traveled incessantly, and each of us found problems in police training that neither had known about. In one case it was that trainees had no ammunition for live-fire training. In another, that equipment distribution was not keeping up, so trainees were being sent back from training without full uniforms, or sometimes even weapons. Over time I realized that there were common human elements contributing to these problems.

One is that people don't like reporting to their superiors that they cannot fix a problem. Especially if there is a continuing discussion,

---

[1] In Afghanistan, more than 20 working groups were formed of all the international donors and the relevant Afghan ministries for each major subject area such as power, agriculture, finance.

there is a tendency to think or hope that resolution will be reached in another meeting, another week, a week after that, and so on. So problems don't come up the chain of command, leaders are irritated, and, much worse, time is lost. The problem is magnified when difficulties need to be reported across institutional lines. USAID officers instinctively don't want to pass decisionmaking to political levels of the Embassy. Military officers would rather not hand off a problem to civilians. And contractors have no incentive to tell the contracting agency that things are not working, or to report problems that are not directly part of the contract responsibility, e.g., that equipment whose delivery is outside the training contract responsibility isn't arriving.

In many cases, the failure to report problems promptly is neither deliberate nor the result of a failure in supervision. Rather, it is more likely an instinctive behavior that goes unchallenged because it is unexamined. In any event, the question is what to do about it? Yelling, pleading, lecturing, and cajoling down the chain of command all gave limited results. In some circumstances, the "can do" approach of the military may also make it difficult to recognize that some difficulties are not "challenges" but, rather, problems that need a solution from higher up.

Our current management technique focuses on extensive matrices of factors that need to be tracked. The matrices are supposed to reveal problems in progress toward assigned benchmarks. Sometimes this works, but the systems I have seen used in Iraq and Afghanistan suffer from a number of problems. They too often measure inputs rather than outputs; and the latter can be enormously difficult to define. They tend to focus excessively on what can be measured and exclude subjective judgments. As multiple "indicators" are combined for presentation higher up the chain of command, they become increasingly strategic and general, obscuring particular problems that may need command attention. And for Embassy and USAID operations, the data management of a really complex matrix requires staff support that frequently is not available.

One possible solution for economic donor coordination occurred to me too late in my Afghan tour to really try it out. Hence, I suggest it while noting that it is not a proven principle. My proposal is to institute a requirement that problems not fixed within a specific time, say 30 days, must be reported. Since not every problem is worth raising to the top, a small cell would evaluate each month's set of problems and recommend which ones needed to be reported to the Ambassador. The Ambassador would not necessarily try to solve them all, but could decide which ones needed to be taken to higher levels of the host government, worked on with other nations' senior leaders, or dealt with across agency or military command lines[2]. More rapidly identifying multinational disagreements leads to the next issue. Once you know the problem, what do you do about it?

International operations; leading from behind

The United States has natural leadership qualities: the size of our budgets and staffs, and frequently the forces or personnel we contribute to a multinational or multi-donor process. But with those attributes can come resentment and problems. One is in the nature of international coordination, be it in military alliances or civilian donor enterprises. When operations are messy and results are imperfect, often there are calls for a unified strategy or a single coordinator. These responses have value, but their ability to provide a solution is frequently exaggerated.

In slightly oversimplified terms, a strategy is a series of linked steps, actions, or maneuvers to achieve one or more objectives. Strategies are broad statements and have to be handed off for implementation to a commander, a CEO, or some other leader to make and execute hundreds or thousands of decisions. In a corporation or an army the chain of command is clear. In multinational operations it is not. Nations will accept a certain amount of guidance, but they won't take orders. Worse still, when it comes to development and diplomacy, many nations do not have even a unified national chain of command. The development departments of most European nations are separate from the foreign ministries, and very explicitly do not take orders from them. British troops in Afghanistan may be fighting in Helmand Province, but the British aid agency, the Department for International Development, reports to London, not to the NATO/ISAF commander, and not to the British Ambassador in Kabul. Germany's large police-training mission

---

[2] Embassy Kabul, like Baghdad, now has an Ambassadorial rank deputy for economic and assistance affairs who could frequently replace the Ambassador in the role I describe.

reports to the Ministry of the Interior and depends for trainers on voluntary contributions from the German *Länder*, or states. Multiple nations implementing a strategy can coordinate only through mutual agreement. Coordination can be particularly frustrating for the United States when it supplies the majority of the resources but cannot get all the international actors to pull in one direction. Efforts to go it alone, compel obedience, or just ignore other troop contributors and donors have not been particularly successful and have bred resentment and impeded progress.

While institutional solutions, strategic refinements, and appointment of coordinators have their place, they do not fill the need for the myriad of detailed decisions required in the field. However, a combination of problem solving and leading from behind make it possible to improve performance, although not to cure the underlying problem.

Because of its size, the United States often has a broader view of issues than many other nations. In Afghanistan, USAID officers are present in every one of the international/Afghan working groups, although we do not lead every one. If we use our breadth of knowledge, we can often provide leadership without causing offense. Two examples from Afghanistan stand out.

One was in electrical power transmission and generation. We were one of several donors building a large electrical transmission system to bring power from several central Asian states to Kabul. We became aware of problems caused by a lack of coordination between donors and between Afghan ministries. We produced an interagency discussion paper detailing our understanding of the problems and recommendations for solution. Next, we passed the paper to the UN, and the head of the UN Assistance Mission in Afghanistan (UNAMA) convened a meeting of the parties involved, the Ambassadors from the United States, India, and Germany, and the heads of the World Bank and Asian Development Bank teams. Together we worked out a consensus position embodying most of our recommendations. We were then able to take a unified approach to the Afghan government that over a number of months brought about changes.

Working in this way, we avoided creating the impression that the United States was trying to order others around. We were able to build and maintain consensus and, most importantly, get results. We repeated the pattern in dealing with the question of which ministries should have priority of international effort for building their internal staff capacity, although in that case we were able to reach consensus at a lower level. This approach enabled us to build greater authority for the UN and get more cooperation from other donors than if we had convened the meetings or simply gone unilaterally to the Afghan government with views different from those of the other donors. Not every situation can be met in this way, but the approach of flagging problems and proposing solutions, but letting others lead, can often be effective and should be used more frequently. When it turns out that policy changes or resources are needed from national capitals, this approach also results in different national representatives all recommending the same solution to their superiors. Because national governments tend to give deference to the views of their own representatives on the ground, this approach is often more effective than having the issue pressed unilaterally by Washington at the level of capitals.

Planning and coordination; hindrance as well as help

Proper planning and coordination are so broadly accepted as essential to effectiveness that to suggest they can also cause problems borders on the sacrilegious. Yet, it is so. In Afghanistan, and to some extent in Iraq, the number of effective national officials is small. There are direct tradeoffs between how much they can be involved in planning and getting things accomplished. Large, international staffs, all clamoring for national counterparts and participation in planning groups, can drown limited local staffs so that everyone is planning and no one is executing.

Further, because the locals have limited personnel, the foreigners often do the planning and then try to "sell" the results. Sometimes this works, but often I observed that we had ignored local political problems, neglected local preferences for how they wanted to solve a problem, or decided to solve problems that the locals were not concerned about. Because we control the funds, we can often drive agreement in principle. But without real acceptance of both problem and solution, much of what we were funding was destined to remain either unworkable or unfinished. Sewerage systems that never connected to houses, power plants without a continuing source of fuel, and administrative structures that remained ineffective because they had not resolved issues of local power litter the landscape in Iraq and Afghanistan. Highly paid foreign advisors often provided advice better suited to America than Iraq. And a proliferation of technical advisors from multiple donors sometimes provided conflicting advice that left the locals either confused or picking the advice that best suited extrinsic political concerns.

There is no perfect solution to these dilemmas, but some bits of advice can be offered.

On the broad level, look carefully at how much coordination and planning is essential. The United States has built the world's greatest economy on a decentralized basis, yet Americans are remarkably given to central planning when helping others develop their economies. Before starting new planning mechanisms or expanding existing ones, consider closely—in dialogue with the locals—whether they agree with the need and can hold up their end of the exercise.

On a more detailed level, spend a lot of time discussing with the locals their conception of their problems. Far too often I have seen us try to push solutions before we have agreement on the problem. Local officials have a tendency to agree to our proposals because we have power and money, but this does not always mean they intend to implement the plan. Substantial time for building relationships may be necessary before one has an adequate grasp of local views on a problem; not only its technical nature but the political or social factors that may be involved.

A final point, although there could be many more: stop using PowerPoint presentations unless absolutely required. Non-native English speakers may be having trouble dealing with language or translation. Putting a PowerPoint presentation in front of them simply divides attention and reduces comprehension. Conceptual diagrams, of which we seem increasingly enamored, are frequently meaningless across cultural lines, lead to more confusion than clarity, and cause disagreement through misunderstanding.

Lessons learned for implementation will no doubt fill volumes and will always be influenced by specific circumstances. Yet I hope that these reflections on a few common problems and possible solutions will be useful.

Essay 18

Beyond the Cold War: Pakistan and Somalia

By Robert B. Oakley

I would like to offer lessons learned from two complex operations in which I was involved in the late 1980s and early 1990s. The first was in Pakistan—linked to Afghanistan then as now by Islam, tribal connections, and cross-border war—in the final years of the Cold War, when the Soviet Union was beginning to come apart at the seams, in some measure because of the strain of occupying Afghanistan. The second was in Somalia immediately after the end of the Cold War, when U.S. policymakers expected to reap a "peace dividend." Years later, conflict continues in both areas.

Pakistan

During the first 3 years of the Carter administration, U.S. policy toward Pakistan was dominated by concerns about nuclear proliferation, in large measure because of legislation that imposed sanctions against non-nuclear states attempting to develop nuclear weapons.[1] In April 1979, the Carter Administration imposed military and economic sanctions on Pakistan after determining that it was

---

[1] The Indian detonation of a "peaceful nuclear explosive" in 1974 had caused Pakistan to accelerate its program to develop nuclear weapons. The U.S. Government generally, and the Congress in particular, were alarmed by the prospect of a new nuclear arms race. The 1977 Glenn Amendment to the Foreign Assistance Act of 1961 prohibited U.S. assistance to any non-nuclear weapon state (as defined by the 1967 Nuclear Non-Proliferation Treaty). The 1978 Nuclear Nonproliferation Act prohibited the export of nuclear technology to non-nuclear weapon states that did not accept full International Atomic Energy Agency safeguards and threatened sanctions against any state that attempted to acquire unsafeguarded technology.

constructing a uranium enrichment facility. After the Soviet invasion of Afghanistan in December 1979, President Carter offered to resume military and economic aid, but Pakistan initially declined the offer. With the approval of Congress, the United States resumed military assistance for Pakistan.

Throughout the 1980s, American policy toward Pakistan continued to be dominated by opposition to the Soviet occupation of Afghanistan, despite concerns about Pakistan's ambitions to become a nuclear power—and constant congressional pressure to enforce sanctions. Pakistan became the linchpin in President Reagan's Cold War confrontation with the USSR, and his administration consistently certified to Congress that Pakistan did not possess nuclear weapons.

American involvement in the war in Afghanistan was massive but indirect. The fighting was done by Afghans and Muslim volunteers. Training and materiel were supplied through the Pakistani Inter-Services Intelligence (ISI). The United States embraced the use of Islam to inspire and reinforce the Afghan mujahedeen and supported Saudi efforts to recruit thousands of volunteers from everywhere in the Muslim world for the fight to liberate Afghanistan, Many of the volunteers looked beyond Afghanistan to liberation of Soviet Central Asia. To promote its fundamentalist version of Islam, known as wahhabism, Saudi Arabia established hundreds of mosques and Islamic schools in the Pakistan-Afghanistan border area. These Saudi efforts, combined with ISI and CIA military assistance, eventually gave rise to Al Qaeda, which gained strength in Afghanistan in the mid to late 1980s.

On August 18, 1988, Zia-ul-Haq, President of Pakistan and Army Chief of Staff, and U.S. Ambassador Arnold Raphel were killed in an airplane crash that was apparently the result of sabotage. No one really knew what or who was behind the crash. Because Pakistan was funneling massive amounts of U.S. support to the Afghan mujahedeen, the USSR was an easy suspect. India was another. The Pakistani political leadership saw enemies everywhere. President Reagan responded immediately, sending a high-level delegation led by Secretary of State Schultz to attend Zia's funeral on August 20. The delegation included CENTCOM Commander George Crist, Assistant Secretary of Defense Richard Armitage, senior members of Congress, and myself, the new ambassador. By the time the planes reached Pakistan, my appointment had been confirmed by the Senate.

During the flight we developed a strategy and a series of steps and resources required to achieve its objectives. Our top priority was to reassure Pakistan and its potential adversaries (the USSR, India, and Afghanistan) that the United States was prepared to provide any assistance required to secure Pakistan's stability and territorial integrity. More specific U.S. objectives were to ensure continued support of the mujahedeen, stop further development of the Pakistani nuclear program, see to it that the elections Zia had promised for September 1988 were held, and stabilize Pakistan. The key to achieving these objectives was Pakistan's Army, and its new leadership. The U.S. plan included the supply of new weapons systems, spare parts, and training. This step required lifting sanctions applied by the Carter Administration. By the end of 1989, all sanctions had been lifted, and the United States was providing hundreds of millions of dollars to the Afghan Mujahedeen via the CIA and the ISI.

Within a year, circumstances in the region changed radically, as did American policy. In early 1990, tensions mounted with India over violent confrontations in Kashmir. Pakistan was strained by the presence of 3–5 million Afghan refugees, and suspension of American military and economic assistance was imminent. The Soviet Union had withdrawn from Afghanistan, and pressures for U.S. sanctions against Pakistan were increasing. The Pakistani Army leadership decided to reactivate the nuclear weapons program, despite U.S. warnings that this step would block all U.S. military and economic assistance. On October 1, 1990, President Bush stated that he could no longer certify that Pakistan did not possess nuclear weapons. The United States stopped all assistance, including delivery of F-16s already paid for, unintentionally causing Pakistan to turn to North Korea for ballistic missiles in exchange for nuclear assistance. The now infamous A. Q. Khan network was involved in many such operations throughout the 1980s and 1990s and beyond.

The U.S. withdrawal of military and economic support infuriated all Pakistanis, not just the military and ISI. Anti-American sentiment also arose among the mujahedeen, who were abandoned by the United States upon Soviet withdrawal from Afghanistan. More than a decade of war had ravaged the Afghan economy and armed much of the populace. Factional fighting among the mujahedeen increased, which created political and military opportunities for the Taliban. Throughout Afghanistan and Pakistan, and especially along the border of the two countries, Islamist extremism and anti-Americanism flourished and were exploited by the Taliban and, later, al Qaeda, which came to dominate the Taliban.

Somalia

Serious U.S. involvement in Somalia started in the late 1970s, also as a result of the Cold War. The Soviets were providing major military support to Ethiopia and were seen by U.S. policymakers, especially National Security Adviser Zbigniew Brzezinski, as preparing to overrun Somalia. Because Somalia's strategic location could enable the Soviets to block the vital shipping lanes bringing oil from the Persian Gulf, the United States began setting up a string of bases (or military operating facilities) along the periphery of the Indian Ocean (Kenya, Oman, Somalia). The United States provided large-scale military and economic assistance to Somalia, despite the dictator Siad Barre's horrendous human rights record.

After the end of the Cold War, the Soviets stopped their support for Ethiopian dictator Mengistu Haile Mariam, and the United States cut back sharply on assistance to Somalia. Civil war broke out in 1991, and Siad Barre fled the country. He was replaced by several clan-based "warlords," who fought each other. This internal conflict made it almost impossible to grow food in Somalia's "bread basket." The food shortage was compounded by 3 years of severe drought. The ensuing famine caused probably 300,000–400,000 civilian deaths. International efforts to provide food were unsuccessful; the warlords either blocked delivery or seized the food for their own purposes. Perhaps for the first time, such immense human suffering was brought by television into our living rooms. President George H. W. Bush felt a deep humanitarian commitment, and Congress and the American people overwhelmingly favored American action to relieve the suffering.

A small UN peacekeeping force of lightly armed Pakistanis sent to Somalia was a total failure. This led President Bush in late November 1992 to endorse an option proposed by DOD to deploy urgently a multinational force (MNF) built around a core of two U.S. divisions under U.S. command but approved by the United Nations Security Council (UNSC). President Bush and his very experienced national security team (who had up to 12 years in office)—including the U.S. Central Command, which had operational command of the MNF (UNITAF)—had a very good understanding of what was likely to succeed, and what limits should be placed on U.S. operations (applying the Weinberger-Powell doctrine). They were realists, while committed to an idealistic mission. The United States had no interest in Somalia other than humanitarian.

President Bush was a "lame duck" and did not believe he could commit the United States to long-term political or economic obligations. Nation-building would be up to the next President and Congress. Troops from 20 other countries (10,000 personnel) also participated. France, Italy, Canada, and Belgium sent combat forces that reinforced the overall military capability of UNITAF. A number of African and Arab Forces participated, primarily for political reasons. These governments wanted to be part of the rescue effort for an African Muslim state, but did not really have the capability or will to fight. However, they did make U.S. forces more acceptable.

The U.S. mission was to stop violence, get the International humanitarian assistance flowing, and prepare the way for a follow-up UN Force and a UN Special Representative to take on the larger humanitarian task of nation-building.

I was selected by President Bush and his national security team, several of whom I had worked for previously, to operate in tandem with USMC Lt Gen Bob Johnson. One of the lessons President Bush's team had learned from U.S. defeats in Vietnam and Lebanon was that effective diplomacy and political actions could help military forces avoid potentially costly casualties. I got to Mogadishu on December 9, 1992, with a small but experienced staff; my DCM had been with me in 1973, and the USAID Disaster Assistance Response Team (DART) had been in the country for almost a year. General Johnson and I virtually integrated our staffs; my DCM became his POLAD, and he appointed USMC BrigGen Tony Zinni to work directly with me.

We were in constant communication and agreed that the first option in dealing with the warlords would be dialogue backed up by threat and, very rarely, the use of military force. The UNITAF commander, Lt Gen Johnson, paid particular attention to establishing a single chain of command for UNITAF. Each national contingent was assigned a particular geographic region (there were eight, plus Mogadishu). Each had U.S. liaison officers and their own liaison officers at UNITAF headquarters. The contingents that were not combat-capable were assigned to guard the Mogadishu airport and port and military and humanitarian installations, such as warehouses. All contingents were happy to serve under U.S. command. There was full unity of effort.

This approach of giving dialogue primacy over the use of force proved successful. By February 1993, warlord violence had largely ceased. All heavy weapons were impounded subject to UNITAF inspection. International organizations and non-governmental organizations were providing food and medical assistance for the very large population of Mogadishu and most of the southern parts of the country, where the famine had hit the hardest. The Chairman of the Joint Chiefs of Staff, Colin Powell, in accordance with the original plan, initiated the phased removal of U.S. forces in preparation for the deployment of the new, much larger UN force (UNOSOM II). The UNSC appointed a new Special Representative, Admiral John Howe, who was selected by the new President, Bill Clinton, to demonstrate strong U.S. support for UNOSOM II. I went back into retirement.

President Clinton and the civilian members of his national security team had no experience—or no recent experience—with national security matters, and their relations with the uniformed military were strained. They also had no previous experience in nation-building or in dealing with a situation as complicated as Somalia. However, a major theme of Bill Clinton's campaign had been the rebuilding of failed states, greater use of the United Nations, and the spread of democracy. Somalia seemed the perfect place to put theory into practice.

Accordingly, the United States led the UNSC into a drastic change of mission for UNOSOM II: it would have the tasks both of building new democratic political institutions and rebuilding an economy that had been totally destroyed. A large, colonial-type UN infrastructure was envisioned for the entire country, not only the southern half. The warlords were to be disarmed—by military force, if necessary. They were to be told what to do, not consulted. And all of this with a much weaker military force that would contain no U.S. units. There was provision for a small, separate, U.S. Quick Reaction Force (QRF) that could be used to assist UNOSOM II if it ran into serious trouble, but that force was not in the UNOSOM chain of command.

It was not long before this new UN approach led to political confrontation with the most powerful warlord in Mogadishu, Mohamed Farrah Aidid. Aidid had played a leading role in ousting Siad Barre and had aspirations to take his place. He also had a profound distrust of UN Secretary General Boutros-Gali dating back to the latter's tenure as Egypt's Deputy Foreign Minister, when he had strongly supported Siad Barre. The political face-off quickly turned into a military confrontation when UNOSOM sent a small number of Pakistani peacekeepers to inspect the compound in which Aidid's weapons were stored, in accordance with the agreement worked out by UNITAF. The compound was also the site of Aidid's radio station, which he considered essential to his political power. Fearing that this was the first part of a UN plot to destroy him, Aidid ordered his force to attack the Pakistanis, which they did, ruthlessly.

This event quickly led to a new UNSC Resolution (drafted by the United States) that essentially called for UNOSOM II to "get" Aidid. The (unforeseen) consequences of this resolution produced another critical change of mission. The goals of political and economic reconstruction, and even continuing support for humanitarian activities, were subordinated to military action against Aidid and his militia. Over the summer, UNOSOM II launched a number of attacks on Aidid's forces in Mogadishu, none of which accomplished the objectives of capturing Aidid or breaking the back of his force.

The U.S. QRF came to the assistance of UNOSOM II by launching a no-warning helicopter gunship attack on a compound where Aidid's top military and political clan members were conferring. The pot boiled over. Aidid suddenly became the hero of all Somalis, who are by nature very xenophobic. Attacks on UNOSOM II multiplied, and President Clinton felt obliged to come to their help, as well as to find a way to do away with the confrontational Aidid. Aidid had become a domestic political embarrassment.

President Clinton dispatched U.S. Special Operations Forces units to do the job. This operation led to the infamous "Black Hawk Down" incident of October 3–4, in which 18 Americans were killed and 78 wounded. The impact on an unsuspecting Congress (which had not been aware that U.S. forces were engaged in direct combat) and the American people can be likened to a volcanic eruption.

On the ground in Somalia, the large, highly professional, experienced staff commanding the powerful UNITAF—whose top commanders had served in Vietnam, Lebanon, and other operations of a civil-military nature and had conducted exercises in Somalia and Kenya—had been replaced by a small, pick-up staff commanding a much weaker UNOSOM II force. Admiral Howe was an excellent officer, but he had only limited experience abroad, and none at all in Africa. The unity of command that had marked UNITAF had been replaced by a collection of separate national contingents with little cohesion that often relied upon their superiors at home, rather than the UNOSOM II commander, for much of their guidance. Yet the UNOSOM II mission was much more intrusive and confrontational UNITAF. These changes constituted one of the major failures in creating the situation that led to the fateful decision by President Clinton to deploy U.S. forces in an effort to capture or kill Aidid.

Another important factor was the absence of a U.S. interagency body paying full-time attention to Somalia. In the State Department, the only official working full time on Somalia was the Country Director—four echelons down from the Assistant Secretary for Africa. The Department of Defense was following things a bit more closely, but the focus was on withdrawing U.S. forces, and there was little communication with the State Department.

The extremely strong, negative reaction to the Black Hawk Down incident caused a rapid reevaluation of policy by the Clinton Administration. Withdrawal of all remaining U.S. Forces was a given; the only question was timing. After a long, tough meeting with some 20 leaders of Congress, President Clinton was able to obtain a delay of 6 months. This period was to be used to persuade other countries to increase their contingents substantially, with assistance from the United States in weapons and funds, so that UNOSOM II would not leave along with the U.S. forces. A U.S. task force of some 5,000 personnel with aircraft, tanks, helicopters, and other weapons was dispatched to provide protection for the U.S. withdrawal. However, initial plans, approved by the President, for using this force to help UNOSOM II regain and control Mogadishu were cancelled. The President's political advisors did not want to run the risk of even a single casualty. The U.S. withdrawal was completed by the end of March 1993. Despite its reinforcements, UNOSOM II lasted only another year, departing in

March 1994. Somalia had largely returned to the chaotic situation that had prevailed in 1991, with feuding clans and no effective government.

The extreme reluctance to incur casualties for fear of domestic political consequences became the dominant consideration of U.S. policy on humanitarian intervention for the next decade. The United States refused to become involved in stopping genocide in Rwanda. The U.S. intervention in Haiti was conducted with overwhelming force and only suffered two casualties. There were no U.S. casualties in the Bosnia and Kosovo operations. However, the Clinton Administration did organize itself for the orderly conduct of U.S. interventions. New interagency organizations and procedures were developed that worked well for the Somalia withdrawal. One of the new mechanisms was an interagency executive committee at the assistant secretary level that met weekly to assign tasks and monitor ongoing operations. Jim Dobbins at the State Department, Dick Clarke at the NSC, and I were members. I was the co-chair. They worked even better when applied to Haiti. Jim Dobbins describes this very well in his books on nation-building.

U.S. policymakers initially saw these two conflicts in the context of the Cold War and intervened to protect American interests. Military assistance and diplomacy were shaped more by the nature of the Soviet Union than by the nature of the cultures where Cold War battles were waged. With the end of the Cold War, Washington expected to extricate itself from both conflicts, and seemed for a while to have succeeded, but developments in Southwest Asia and the Horn of Africa have drawn the United States back to those regions. The developments are rooted in local cultures, but they have been energized and shaped substantially by past and current U.S. interventions.

Policymakers should absorb the many lessons of American experiences in these two regions—most especially the need to understand and respect the strength of other cultures—when considering whether and how to intervene in any of the troubled areas that are now the objects of our attention. The consequences of intervention are unpredictable, and can persist long beyond the tenure of the officials who initiate military operations.

Essay 19

Every Complex Operation Needs a BG Rich Ellis[1]

By Thomas W. O'Connell

As a participant in Operation *Urgent Fury,* (Grenada, October 1983), I was stunned by the lack of clarity in strategic, operational, and tactical mission orders and intelligence provided to tactical forces. From the super-quick Phase One through Phase Four set points, each operational phase suffered from:

- poor human intelligence (HUMINT),

- a lack of clear estimates on enemy (Cuban and Grenadian) dispositions and intentions,

- confusing and imprecise mission orders, and

---

[1] BG Rich Ellis, USA, died suddenly in May 2009, and a Celebration of Life Ceremony was held at Fort Myer Main Chapel in Arlington, VA, on 29 May. Attendees included the current Director, Central Intelligence Agency (CIA), The Honorable Leon Panetta, the former Director CIA, General Mike Hayden, USAF (Ret), the Director, National Security Agency, LTG Keith Alexander, USA, and Director of Intelligence, Joint Staff, MG, Mike Flynn, USA. Speakers included the Director of the National Intelligence Community Staff, LTG Jeff Kimmons, USA, LTG Rick Zahner, USA, Army G2, (who served as escort officer), former XVII Airborne Corps Commander, LTG(R), USA, John Vines (who served in Iraq as a Corps Commander with BG Ellis as his G2), MG (R), USA Barb Fast, who served several tours with BG Ellis, Army G2 SES Gerry Turnbow, and Sergeant Major Gary Creclius, USA of Fort Bragg who put a perfect relationship with soldiers into sharp perspective. All joined many hundred celebrants to pay tribute to Rich, Ms. Meri Ellis and their two sons, one a newly commissioned ROTC officer. Rich never got to pin on his bars.

149

- overconfidence in the joint interoperability of participating forces.

Launched in the immediate wake of the Beirut Marine Corps barracks bombing, the first priority for conventional forces in *Urgent Fury* seemed to be to prevent a similar explosive ramming of the 82d Airborne Division Command Post established in the partially completed terminal at Point Salinas Airport after Army Ranger forces had seized the airfield with a parachute assault. Airborne manpower was heavily committed to this initial task, as Rangers, and Marines along with Special Operations Forces completed initial combat tasks around the island.

Although the pre-assault national intelligence collection activities conducted on the island were lauded as heroic and effective by some in Washington, the Special Operations personnel charged with early entry and target-specific assaults knew this was not the case. Several died and many were wounded as operations went awry. Later, 82d Airborne aviators and paratroopers were killed in a tactical insertion accident during an unnecessary air assault on a nonexistent enemy force. My battalion had five paratroopers wounded when a Navy A-7 strafed a hilltop where a U.S. soldier had inadvertently fired a burst of anti-aircraft fire from an abandoned enemy antiaircraft artillery piece near our position.

Despite these incidents, all objectives were seized, the medical students at True Blue Campus were rescued, the Cuban construction forces (about 780 in number, with about 45 actual Cuban military) were dispatched or captured, and resisting Grenada forces (both People's Revolutionary Army and Grenadian militia) were quickly eliminated. Numerous hostile embassies were closed, with "diplomats" sent packing. Civilian casualties and collateral damage were minimal.

For almost 20 years before Grenada, U.S. Atlantic Command had conducted contingency scenarios for the Nation's Rapid Reaction Force, (XVIII Airborne Corps). SOLID SHIELD alternated Command Post and Field Training Exercises on a yearly basis. The types of operational scenarios were very much like the Operation *Urgent Fury* OPLAN. A review of the after action reports (AAR) of these exercises would provide an accurate template for constructing an AAR of Operation *Urgent Fury*.

Typically, these reports start out at company and battalion level and tend to be brutally honest. The soldiers that draft them went through all the sweat and exhaustion of the ground phases and are not shy about pointing out shortcomings. As the reports are edited at brigade, division, and corps levels, they tend to become pabulum, with the bottom line reading "we did this well." In my experience, every lesson from *Urgent Fury* had already been well documented in previous SOLID SHIELD AARs.

This deficit was not unique to Grenada. In Haiti, Panama, Iraq, Afghanistan, Colombia, the Philippines, Lebanon, and any number of counterterrorist operations, our ability to put key assets on the ground or have them in place, in my experience, has been less than optimal. Quite simply, we owe our forces a better effort.

A quarter-century after *Urgent Fury,* we find the nation in conflicts that have lasted longer than WWII. As these conflicts persist, the nation must stand ready to conduct worldwide, short-notice, complex operations like *Urgent Fury*. Those operations might be executed *in* the current theaters of major conflict, Iraq and Afghanistan, or in neighboring countries. Options might include: attack and defeat of a massed or trapped insurgent or terrorist force, killing or capturing a High Value Individual, interdiction of a nuclear weapon (or related) shipment, destruction of a known piracy base, resolution of a hostage barricade situation, strike at an insurgent sanctuary, recovery of MANPADS, vessel recovery, etc.

Our military and intelligence forces are certainly in a better position now to execute complex operations than at perhaps any time in history. Battle-hardened, experienced in diverse theaters, and justifiably confident in their joint capabilities, today's forces enjoy many benefits from our recent operations:

- (many) Combatant Command Staffs are accomplished operators,

- communications are more robust and capable,

- persistent intelligence, surveillance, and reconnaissance is flexible, more available, and capable,

- logistics procedures and routes are well established around the world,

- specific contingency authorizations are in place to streamline response times and enable quick approval for launching operations,

- operating arrangements with allied forces are better understood and practiced, and interagency operations are enhanced through significantly improved cooperation.

I see much hope for future improvement in solving the quest for those critical last minute operational and intelligence requirements. New authorities have been granted to our forces that allow recruitment and training of surrogates. Thus far, I have not addressed the general officer mentioned in the title, BG Richard Ellis. In the course of our respective careers, we often had occasion to look at recent operations or ongoing problems and discuss "what ifs". As intelligence officers, often supporting Special Operations Forces, we were familiar with the demands for access to target areas, precise intelligence on opposition threats, and the problems associated with providing information on last minute changes in the tactical situation. In assessing needs for US forces in what was once called the Global War on Terrorism, we discussed the incredibly diverse requirements placed on our intelligence systems and operatives.

In later discussions with BG Ellis at his CIA Community Staff office, we talked about the need for a network against the network. For decades, members of our Special Forces trained and fought with numerous allies in all theaters. We have a magnificent corps of potential operatives that can easily access key areas of operational interest with minimal risk. Many of these retired or separated soldiers would gladly volunteer to help the United States with our current global conflicts. Obtaining agreement from donor countries would be possible in many cases. BG Ellis' exceptional range of critical assignments combined with his HUMINT skills allowed him to envision the wisdom of such a program. He knew the value of an offensive program designed to put unrelenting pressure on an enemy that often enjoys freedom of action and movement. His experiences in Korea, Iraq, SOUTHCOM, Europe, Special Mission Units, Special Forces, Army Intelligence, and the CIA placed him in a position where few U.S. officers could match his insight and imagination with respect to complex operations. Success in the future likely will demand many more officers like him. Moreover, a network of capable clandestine operatives would be equally valuable and essential in supporting complex operations. General Ellis was routinely pressed during his career to come up with immediate solutions to overwhelming demands from combat forces in "crunch time'. The risk of establishing such a network would be minimal, the potential payoff could be immense. We can do this and do it now. Surely, in the not too distant future, a young intelligence officer in a key position will be searching for answers he wished he had. He will be wondering what he could do with a force envisioned by Rich Ellis.

The swiftness of a developing crisis with attendant complexity can overwhelm policy officials and commanders alike. Establishing this network now would be a fitting tribute to his legacy. Reflecting back on *Urgent Fury*, a BG Rich Ellis would certainly have had a different approach to the intelligence aspects of the problem. The benefits of his vision and tireless efforts against our adversaries should be embraced and focused on the sudden emergencies that will continue to challenge the nation and our allies.

Post-Conflict Reconstruction Challenges: Some Observations from Iraq

By Robin Raphel

T he challenges to post-conflict reconstruction that I address here cover both processes and programs. They are drawn primarily from my experience working on the U.S. reconstruction effort in Iraq between 2003 and 2007, first as an advisor to the Ministry of Trade and Coordinator of Ministerial Advisors for the Coalition Provisional Authority, then as the Department of State Coordinator for Iraq Reconstruction, and finally as the Deputy Special Inspector General for Iraq Reconstruction.

Finding the most appropriate partner for U.S. reconstruction assistance efforts. USAID and other traditional aid institutions, concerned about legal frameworks and often still bound by established procedures, have been rightly criticized for automatically seeking a host-government partner with which to sign a traditional assistance agreement. Post-conflict governments are inherently weak—ministers have fled and bureaucrats have disappeared, whether in reaction to new policies (de-Baathification, in the case of Iraq) or the general disruption of war. Going directly to individual ministries can work; in Iraq, the Ministry of Oil remained competent, if thinly staffed. The Ministry of Health, on the other hand, was plagued with problems. Waiting for bureaucracies and governments to reinvent themselves (or, worse still, be reinvented by outsiders) can take an unacceptable amount of time when citizens are expecting rapid improvement in their lives. Local communities may articulate their immediate, local priorities, but when it comes to providing basic social services, they often need to be tied into the national level system—the power grid, the canal system, the national school and health systems—which requires professional staff and supplies.

Thus, we need to look for other partners. NGOs that are still functioning can often be useful partners in meeting local needs. The conceptual answer to identifying the right partner lies in finding an entity that can get things done and understands what is appropriate for local communities and what is inherently in the purview of the national or provincial government. Post-conflict assistance teams need to work with groups that can repair schools and clinics, but know not to build new ones unless it is clear they will be supported by the government in due course; help power plants get back up and running, but not order new generators that local technicians cannot maintain; repair existing water and irrigation facilities, but not plan new ones that could disrupt a fragile water table; and, finally, can assist communities to improve community life in very local ways—building parks, digging wells, etc.

Ensuring local buy-in and avoiding aid dependency. Much has been written about the need to have local understanding and support for assistance projects and programs. We know about the clinics and schools built in Iraq that had no staff because they were not part of the national ministry staffing plan (which provided all the government doctors, nurses, and teachers countrywide) or were in dangerous neighborhoods where local people dared not travel. These problems could have been avoided by taking the time to find people in the ministries in charge of staffing and placement of facilities. Similarly, costly mistakes about the types of power generators, buildings that were too high for the modest pressure in Iraqi water pipes, imported flour that was unsuitable for baking Iraqi bread, etc., could have been avoided by consulting with Iraqi officials.

The excuse often offered for not consulting the Iraqis was that "we did not have time." This is a fallacy. Rushing to spend reconstruction resources without proper consultation with the Iraqis wasted resources, and often the process was ultimately slower, and certainly less effective. We need to avoid the tendency to do things ourselves when they are not done by local officials or citizens on our timetable. Pushing aside the locals is unwise, even when it applies to simple procedural matters—getting badges for access to the Green Zone, obtaining travel documents, gaining access to computers, furniture, cars, and gasoline. In an effort to expedite all things, U.S. personnel made Iraqis dependent on them, the result of which was simmering resentment among Iraqis at the humiliation of not being able to do the most basic things themselves, or a passive, do-nothing, "let the American take care of it" attitude.

Procedures need to be developed early on to give local officials and citizens the wherewithal and responsibility to manage their basic affairs. This may take more time on the front end of the reconstruction process, but the payoff from people having ownership of projects and programs earlier in the process would be enormous.

Finding the appropriate focus for governance programs: the Center vs. Provincial/regional institutions. As U.S. assistance officials entered Iraq in early 2003, they were under instructions to strengthen local and regional institutions as part of an overall effort to ensure that another strongman would not emerge in Baghdad. This was understandable, given what the autocratic regime of Saddam Hussein had done to Iraq and its people. But in fact, Iraq had been a centralized state for decades. To make it function required restoring national institutions, not just "empowering" provincial politicians, many of whom had little experience in governance and were more interested in the perks of power than the work. Soon the focus was changed to capacity development in the national ministries. At the same time, we wanted to be able to spend money more quickly and visibly at the local level. So, we began to coach newly established provincial assemblies on developing budget priorities and building consensus on a reconstruction budget for the provinces. All these activities were legitimate. But the key to successful assistance to a country is to balance central and regional assistance in a way that respects the established division of labor between the central and regional governments. That division of labor is different in Iraq than in, say, Afghanistan, where the national government has never reached much beyond the capital. In Iraq, the national government had run the food rationing system, the petroleum industry, and other sectors, all of which were crucial to progress in the reconstruction effort.

Promoting constructive civilian-military cooperation in the field. This issue has been much discussed, but it is not yet clear that we have reached practical conclusions. On the positive side, military and civilian officials in the field have come to appreciate what each brings to the table, and in some ways they even attempt to emulate each other. Military officers now regularly seek cultural context and study tribes and customs. Civilians wear combat boots and seek to learn to plan like their military colleagues, and adopt their pervasive acronyms. The demand for political advisors seems insatiable—easily ten percent of the Foreign Service could be employed as POLADS. At the same time, the military complains about being forced to do civilian tasks because the civilians do not "come to the fight." The State Department has scrambled to avoid this criticism, raiding other Foreign Service posts, offering costly incentives for service in Iraq and Afghanistan, and hiring hundreds of temporary employees. Results are mixed. Temporary hires often find it difficult to operate in a government bureaucracy, and in any case in their numbers do not begin to bridge the gap between military and civilian resources. The difference in scale is simply too vast. There will still be 20 colonels breathing down the neck of every civilian reconstruction manager, ready to take on the task if it is not finished in accordance with the often unrealistic timetable of their commanding officer. Even with the plans in train for a civilian reserve, the civilians will always be the smaller player. The sooner that fact is accepted, the sooner we can focus on ensuring that everyone, civilian and military alike, plays to their comparative advantage. No matter how much civilians and military officers try to learn how the other works, the differences in training, experience, resources, and mission will make it difficult for one to effectively replace the other. The overall message should be, "vive la difference"!

How to more effectively promote the rule of law and fight corruption. Rule of law programs in Iraq were the subject of persistent bureaucratic infighting and harsh rhetoric by critics of the reconstruction effort. There was an active debate about who should be in charge—the Department of State's Bureau of Narcotics and Law Enforcement, which had traditionally managed police training? The Department of Justice, which was training judges and court officials, and with some logic saw itself as arbiter of legal programs? USAID, which managed substantial funds for rule of law programs? The Regime Crimes Liaison Office, which had the mission to hunt down and try Saddam-era officials? The result of the infighting was perpetual confusion, and wasted time and resources. The casual observer found it difficult to understand what "rule of law" really meant. Was it shorthand for building prisons for the thousands of new detainees Coalition forces were picking up, and creating courts and judges to try them? Or was it police training, which in Iraq quickly took second place behind training the army? Or was stamping out corruption, which one Iraqi minister dubbed "the second insurgency?"[1]

The Iraq experience demonstrates the need to: 1) clarify and articulate the purpose of various parts of the rule of law mission, 2) prioritize rule of law activities in line with host-country needs, recognizing that this is likely to mean putting more effort into neighborhood policing and arbitration of basic grievances at the expense of training the army and trying alleged terrorists, 3) concerning corruption, be realistic about the time it takes to establish the procedures and transparency that lessen the temptation of corrupt practices, avoid rhetoric that cannot be matched by effective action, and build on existing institutions rather than create new, unfamiliar institutions.

Managing risk. In the early days in Iraq, the environment was relatively safe, and there were few rules, because there was a very limited management structure in the mission. Civilians drove around Baghdad at will, visiting ministries and meeting with counterparts. As security deteriorated and the Mission became more structured, civilian movements were strictly controlled. Insufficient resources for convoys and security details made it difficult to leave the Green Zone to oversee projects and programs. The minimal- or no-risk policy for civilian security has continued to hamper the effective implementation of reconstruction programs in Iraq. The situation was similar regarding reconstruction spending. At first, there was little oversight, but intense public scrutiny and cries of "waste, fraud and abuse" severely undermined the incentive for professionals and contractors to find ways to move money quickly. The no-risk culture needs to be replaced by a risk-management/risk-mitigation culture with respect to both physical

---

[1] To combat corruption, the Coalition created a new Commission on Public Integrity, which competed with established Iraqi institutions as they all traded accusations about corruption within each others' ranks. The first head of this commission, a well intended, apparently honest, but perhaps too eager judge, was eventually driven into exile by progressively more hostile disputes with other oversight organizations. Meanwhile, the man in the street was no closer to getting the basic "justice" he was pleading for.

security for civilian assistance workers and expenditure of assistance funds. It is preferable, for example, to take some risk of corruption or mismanagement in allowing local officials to begin early to manage procurement and other programs, rather than continue to let U.S. officials and their contractors do it all, thereby prolonging the period of dependency—which carries its own high, though unquantifiable, cost.

Toward more appropriate oversight. Under the CPA it was not clear who had authority over what funds (U.S or Iraqi), and thus who had responsibility for overseeing them. The one exception was USAID, which had supplemental funds programmed before the fighting began. USAID arranged for early visits to Iraq by their IG. Funds that were spent by CPA and its home agency, DOD, did not receive much oversight in the early period. Similarly, since the Department of State was not in charge of the Iraq mission, its IG officials did not travel there. The unprecedented $20 billion supplemental appropriation for reconstruction passed in November 2003 provided for a Special Inspector General for Iraq Reconstruction (SIGIR). Starting from scratch and drawing staff from other IG offices and contractors, SIGIR began a process of rapid assessment and reporting on the reconstruction effort that provided much-needed insight into key issues and problems. As time went on, however, agency IGs began to send teams to Iraq, and by 2007 IG teams were bumping into each other all over the country and competing for programs to audit and inspect and potential cases to investigate. Thus, while SIGIR was essential in Iraq in the early years, it became redundant when the agency IGs began to get the funding they needed to operate in Iraq. SIGIR continued to cost the taxpayers close to $30 million each year. It would be more cost-effective for agency IGs to provide oversight to their projects in post-conflict areas from the beginning. They should have the authority and funding to do so.

These observations can be summed up in a few simple concepts.

- Patience is essential. New governments, new economic models, new social contracts—all take more time than we seem to be capable of imagining. In fact, Americans have become notorious for their hyperactivity and unrealistic timetables. Some processes simply cannot be compressed. Accepting that fact from the beginning will save considerable energy and reduce frustration.

- Along the same lines, it is helpful to recall the adage often repeated by military engineers: "you can have it fast and good, but not cheap; you can have it cheap and good, but not fast; you can have it fast and cheap, but not good; you can never have it fast, good and cheap." This speaks to the myriad tradeoffs that policymakers and program managers must make on a daily basis. These limitations need to be more broadly appreciated by policymakers and oversight institutions, including the Congress.

- The most effective and sustainable reconstruction and development programs are demand-driven. Designing such programs requires taking the time to listen and understand host-country priorities—not simply supplying advisors and programs preplanned in Washington. An achievable, post-conflict exit strategy begins with strong partnerships with local officials and citizens.

About the Contributors

Lieutenant General David W. Barno, USA (Ret.), served as overall U.S. and coalition commander in Afghanistan from 2003–2005. He commanded over 20,000 U.S. and Coalition forces as part of Operation *Enduring Freedom* with responsibilities across Afghanistan, Pakistan and portions of Uzbekistan and Tajikistan. He is currently Director of the Near East South Asia Center for Strategic Studies at the National Defense University.

Frederick Barton is a senior adviser in the CSIS International Security Program and co-director of its Post-Conflict Reconstruction Project. Previously, Barton served as the chair of the Obama for President Subgroup on Post-Conflict Reconstruction. He has also served as UN deputy high commissioner for refugees in Geneva (1999–2001) and as the first director of the Office of Transition Initiatives at the U.S. Agency for International Development (1994–1999).

Nesreen Barwari is the minister of municipalities and public works in Iraq. She was first named to the post in 2003, the only woman appointed to the 25-member provisional cabinet. She is the top Iraqi official in charge of water treatment, waste management, environmental sanitation, and municipal facilities. She promoted the empowerment of municipal governance and helped the Provincial Coalition Authority in drafting the Local Power Law, which introduced decentralization to Iraq.

Hans Binnendijk is the Vice President for Research and Theodore Roosevelt Chair in National Security Policy at National Defense University (NDU). He is also the founding Director of the Center for Technology and National Security Policy at NDU. He previously served on the National Security Council as Special Assistant to the President and Senior Director for Defense Policy and Arms Control (1999–2001). From 1994 to 1999, Dr. Binnendijk was Director of the Institute for National Strategic Studies at NDU. Prior to that, he was Principal Deputy Director and Acting Director of the State Department's Policy Planning Staff (1993–1994). In academia, Dr.

163

Binnendijk was Director of the Institute for the Study of Diplomacy at Georgetown University (1991–1993) and Deputy Director and Director of Studies at London's International Institute for Strategic Studies and Editor of *Survival* from 1988–1991. He is author or co-author of more than 100 articles, editorials, and reports. His most recent book is *Civilian Surge: Key to Complex Operations*, published by National Defense University Press in 2009.

Ambassador Barbara K. Bodine is a lecturer and diplomat-in-residence at Princeton University's Woodrow Wilson School of Public and International Affairs. She served over 30 years in the Foreign Service, primarily on Arabian Peninsula and Persian Gulf issues. She was ambassador to Yemen from 1997 through August 2001, Deputy Principal Officer in Baghdad during the Iran-Iraq War (1980–1983), in Kuwait as Deputy Chief of Mission during the Iraqi invasion and occupation (1990–1991), and the senior State Department official and the first coalition coordinator for reconstruction in Baghdad and the Central governorates in the spring of 2003. In addition to several assignments in the State Department's Bureau of Near Eastern Affairs, she was Associate Coordinator for Counterterrorism, Director of East African Affairs, Dean of the School of Professional Studies at the Foreign Service Institute, and Senior Advisor for International Security Negotiations and Agreements in the Bureau of Political-Military Affairs.

Ambassador L. Paul Bremer was appointed by President Bush in May 2003 as Presidential Envoy to Iraq and Administrator of the Coalition Provisional Authority. A career diplomat for 23 years, his service spanned eight Presidencies during which he served on four continents and as Special Assistant or Executive Assistant to six Secretaries of State. He was the U.S. Ambassador to the Netherlands and Ambassador-at-large for Counterterrorism before leaving the State Department for 14 years as a businessman, most recently as Chairman and CEO of Marsh Crisis Consulting.

General Peter W. Chiarelli, USA, is the Vice Chief of Staff of the U.S. Army. In his previous assignment, he was the Senior Military Assistant to the Secretary of Defense from March 2007 to August 2008. He commanded the 1st Cavalry Division during Operation *Iraqi Freedom II*, and commanded Multi-National Corps-Iraq. His principal staff assignments have been as the Operations Officer, 1st Cavalry Division; Executive Assistant and later Executive Officer to the Supreme Allied Commander, Commander United States European Command; and as the Director of Operations, Readiness and Mobilization, at Headquarters, Department of the Army.

General Wesley K. Clark, USA (Ret.), served as NATO's Supreme Allied Commander, Europe, 1997–2000, during which he commanded Operation *Allied Force* in Kosovo, which saved 1.5 million Albanians from ethnic cleansing, and NATO's peacekeeping operations in Bosnia. In previous duty, General Clark was the Commander-in-Chief, US Southern Command, 1996–1997, and the J-5, Joint Staff, 1994–96, where he helped plan the 1994 operation in Haiti, helped negotiate an end to the war in Bosnia, and served as the lead author of Joint Vision 2010 for the U.S. Armed Forces. After his retirement in 2000, he became an investment banker, author, commentator, Presidential candidate, educator, and businessman.

Major General Timothy Cross is a retired British Army officer who served as Deputy of the Office of Reconstruction and Humanitarian Assistance in Iraq in 2003. Previously, he served as the Commander Supply of the 1st (UK) Armored Division during Operation *Desert Storm*. He also served on three operational tours in the Balkans during the 1990s, with the UN in Cyprus in 1980, and in Northern Ireland in the 1970s. General Cross retired in 2007.

Ambassador James Dobbins is a Senior Fellow at RAND, where he directs the International Security and Defense Policy Center. He has served the State Department and White House in a number of positions, including Special Assistant to the President for Latin America, Assistant Secretary of State for Europe, and Ambassador to the European Community. He served as the Clinton administration's special envoy for Somalia, Haiti, Bosnia, and Kosovo, and was the Bush administrations first special Envoy for Afghanistan after 9/11.

Ambassador Jan Eliasson is a former UN Special Envoy for Darfur and current Senior Visiting Scholar at USIP. He served as President of the UN General Assembly, Swedish Ambassador to the United States and to the UN, and Swedish Minister for Foreign Affairs. Mr. Eliasson has been Visiting Professor at Uppsala and Göteborg Universities in

Sweden, has authored and coauthored numerous articles and books, and is a frequent lecturer on foreign policy and diplomacy.

James Kunder is a Senior Resident Fellow at the German Marshall Fund of the United States. He advises on international development issues, including the modernization of foreign assistance and the nexus between security and development. Previously, Mr. Kunder served as Acting Deputy Administrator of the U.S. Agency for International Development (USAID). Beginning in July 2004, he served as USAID Assistant Administrator for Asia and the Near East. From July 2002 to July 2004, he was Deputy Assistant Administrator for Asia and the Near East. From January to May 2002, he was Director for Relief and Reconstruction in Afghanistan.

Ambassador Lewis Lucke was the first USAID Mission Director in Iraq, a Senior Foreign Service Officer, and Coordinator for Reconstruction within the Office of Reconstruction and Humanitarian Assistance. Ambassador Lucke served for 26 years with USAID in nine countries, including postings as Mission Director in Iraq, Haiti, Bolivia, and Jordan, and subsequently as USAID Deputy Assistant Administrator for Iraq. As the first USAID Mission Director to Iraq from 2003–2004, he directed a $4.0 billion development and reconstruction portfolio, the largest USAID program in history. He subsequently served as US Ambassador to the Kingdom of Swaziland from 2004–2006. He received USAID's highest award, the Administrator's Distinguished Career Award in 2001, the Presidential Merit Service Award in 2001, USAID's Award for Heroism in 2004, the Secretary of Defense's Award for Exceptional Public Service in 2004, and five USAID Superior Honor or Meritorious Honor Awards.

Brigadier General H.R. McMaster, USA, is the Director of Concept Development and Experimentation at the Army Capabilities Integration Center, U.S. Army Training and Doctrine Command. Previously, BG McMaster served as a senior research associate at the International Institute for Strategic Studies in London, and as Special Assistant to the Commander, Multinational Force Iraq. His command assignments included command of the Third Armored Cavalry Regiment at Fort Carson, Colorado and in Iraq from 2004 to 2006; command of the 1st Squadron, 4th Cavalry, in Schweinfurt, Germany from October 1999 until June 2002; and command of Eagle Troop, Second Armored

Cavalry Regiment, in Bamberg, Germany, and Southwest Asia during Operations *Desert Shield* and *Desert Storm* and the occupation of southern Iraq. He also served as director of the Commander's Advisory Group at U.S. Central Command from 2003 to 2004. He holds a PhD in history from the University of North Carolina at Chapel Hill and served as an assistant professor at the United States Military Academy. He has published numerous works on history and national security affairs, including his award-wining book *Dereliction of Duty*.

Michael Miklaucic is the Director of Research, Information and Dissemination at the Center for Complex Operations (CCO) at National Defense University. Prior to this assignment he served in various positions at the U.S. Agency for International Development and the Department of State, including service on the Civilian Response Corps Inter-Agency Task Force, as the Senior Program Officer in the USAID Office of Democracy and Governance, and as the Deputy for War Crimes Issues at the Department of State. He received his education from the University of California, the London School of Economics, and the Johns Hopkins University School for Advanced International Studies (SAIS).

Ambassador William Montgomery was U.S. Ambassador to Serbia and Montenegro from 2001–2004 and Chief of Mission to Yugoslavia from 2000–2001. He served as Ambassador to Croatia from 1998 to 2000, Special Advisor to the President for Bosnia in charge of implementation of the Bosnian Peace Plan from 1996–1997, and U.S. Ambassador to Bulgaria. Ambassador Montgomery's career includes tours as an economic-commercial officer in Belgrade, commercial officer in Moscow, political officer in Moscow, and as Deputy Chief of Mission in Dar Es Salaam, as well as assignments in Washington. He was executive assistant to Secretary of State Lawrence Eagleburger and Deputy Secretary of State Clifton Wharton.

Major General William L. Nash, USA (Ret.), was an armored cavalry platoon leader in Vietnam and an armored brigade commander in Operation *Desert* Storm, and commanded the 1st Armored Division from June 1995 to May 1997. MG Nash has extensive experience in peacekeeping operations, both as a military commander in Bosnia-Herzegovina from 1995–1996 and as a civilian administrator for the United Nations in Kosovo in 2000. He was a senior fellow at the

Council on Foreign Relations from 2001–2009. He is also a professorial lecturer at Georgetown University, a visiting lecturer at Princeton University, and a military consultant for ABC News.

Andrew Natsios is a Distinguished Professor in the Practice of Diplomacy at the Edmund Walsh School of Foreign Service at Georgetown University and fellow at the Hudson Institute. From 2001—2006, he served as Administrator of USAID. President Bush also appointed him Special Coordinator for International Disaster Assistance and Special Humanitarian Coordinator for the Sudan. Mr. Natsios also served as U.S. Special Envoy to Sudan from October 2006 to December 2007. His previous service at USAID includes Director of the Office of Foreign Disaster Assistance from 1989–1991 and Assistant Administrator for the Bureau for Food and Humanitarian Assistance (now the Bureau of Democracy, Conflict and Humanitarian Assistance) from 1991–1993. Between 1993 and 1998 he was Vice President of World Vision, the largest faith-based NGO in the world.

Ambassador Ronald E. Neumann is the President of the American Academy of Diplomacy. Ambassador Neumann served as ambassador to Algeria, Bahrain, and Afghanistan. Before Afghanistan, Mr. Neumann served in Baghdad from February 2004 with the Coalition Provisional Authority. Prior to working in Iraq, he was Chief of Mission in Manama, Bahrain, from 2001–2004, Deputy Assistant Secretary in the Bureau of Near East Affairs from 1997–2000 and Director of the Office for Iran and Iraq from 1991–1994.

Robert B. Oakley is a member of the faculty of the Institute for National Strategic Studies at National Defense University. After graduating from Princeton University in 1952, Ambassador Oakley had a distinguished career in the Foreign Service, during which he served in embassies in Abidjan, Saigon, Paris, and Beirut. In 1977 he was named Deputy to the Assistant Secretary of State for East Asia and Pacific Affairs. He served as U.S. Ambassador to Zaire from November 1979 to August 1982, and then became Ambassador to Somalia, where he served until September 1984. Next he became Director of the State Department Office of Combating Terrorism. On January 1, 1987, he was named to the National Security Council Staff as Assistant to the President for Middle East and South Asia, and in August 1988 became Ambassador to Pakistan. In December 1992, President George H. W.

Bush named Ambassador Oakley Special Envoy for Somalia, where he served with Operation *Restore Hope* until March 1993. In October 1993, President Bill Clinton called Ambassador Oakley back to Somalia, where he served until March 1994.

The Honorable Thomas W. O'Connell is an independent defense and intelligence consultant and member of several boards. He served as the Assistant Secretary of Defense for Special Operations and Low Intensity Conflict from 2003–2007. Upon leaving the Pentagon, he received the Department's highest award for civilian service, as well as that of the U.S. Coast Guard. Previously, he served with the Raytheon Corporation for 7 years. Colonel O'Connell's 27-year military career included participation in four conflicts: Vietnam, Grenada, Panama, and Southeast Asia, as well as various assignments to 33 countries. Additionally, he was selected as an original member of the CIA Office of Military Affairs in 1993.

Ambassador Robin Raphel served in the Coalition Provisional Authority in Iraq as Senior Advisor to the Ministry of Trade. She subsequently served as Coordinator for Iraq Reconstruction in the Department of State, and Deputy Inspector General in the office of the Special Inspector General for Iraq Reconstruction. Prior to deploying to Iraq, she was Vice President of the National Defense University. In 1993, Ambassador Raphel became the first Assistant Secretary of State for South Asia. She served as U.S. ambassador to the Republic of Tunisia in the late 1990s. Today she manages the international practice at Cassidy & Associates.

David A. Sobyra is the Acting Director of the Center for Complex Operations (CCO). Mr. Sobyra is a retired Marine Corps aviator and career civil servant in the Office of the Secretary of Defense. He is on detail to NDU from OSD (Policy) in his position with CCO. He has combat experience in Operation *Desert Storm*, served with the Presidential Helicopter Squadron (HMX-1), and, prior to retirement, was the Technology Transfer Branch Chief on the Joint Staff J-5. Mr. Sobyra served with the National Geospatial-Intelligence Agency's Office of International Affairs and Policy from 2003–2004. Prior to assuming Directorship of CCO in May of 2008, he served in OSD (Policy) in the International Security Programs office from 2004–2006, and the Office of Stability Operations Capabilities from 2006–2009.

www.ingramcontent.com/pod-product-compliance
Lightning Source LLC
Chambersburg PA
CBHW080249290526
45790CB00005B/1745